Contents

SOCIAL MEDIA FOR BUSINESS

A Beginner's Guide

Melissa
Perez

Social Media For Business: A Beginner's Guide is also available in accessible formats for people with any degree of visual impairment. The large print edition and e-book (with accessibility features enabled) are available from Need2Know. Please let us know if there are any special features you require and we will do our best to accommodate your needs.

First published in Great Britain in 2013 by
Need2Know
Remus House
Coltsfoot Drive
Peterborough
PE2 9BF
Telephone 01733 898103
Fax 01733 313524
www.need2knowbooks.co.uk

Introduction

Social media is a term used to describe online social interaction. Gone are the days when social media was restricted to a bunch of computer geeks. Today, social media defines success for a business and this makes it important for business owners to know how it works.

When it comes to answering questions like why a business should use social media, the one answer is: it is unavoidable. In the present day, if you want to retain your business, you cannot doubt social media's effectiveness.

A business has to embrace social media one day – be it today, tomorrow or next week. There is no way one can opt out of it. Today, the Internet is believed to be the most reliable means of getting your message across and so, in order to survive the competition and the recent economic meltdown, a business has to leverage the power of social media.

We live in a world where social media has given a new meaning to conducting an online business. The widespread use of this technology has also played a pivotal role in giving ecommerce a much-needed boost. Thanks to social media, it is now possible to purchase everything from a keychain to a car right from the confines of your home. Social media has truly inspired the idea of a world where everything is at your fingertips.

It is important to acknowledge that social media is one of the single most influential forums that can take your business success to a whole new level. When the use of social media for business is in question, there are virtually countless routes you can take which have been explained in depth right here.

As you will continue reading, you will find all about social media types and how a business can use them to its advantage. In addition, strategies to attract target audience and to encourage them into staying with you have also been revealed in this comprehensive guide.

Corporate giants across the globe are making efforts to integrate social media into their marketing campaigns and for good reason. Enterprises are making use of social media as they have acknowledged how effective it can be for a business to fulfil its goals and objectives.

'Out of the 100 companies that made it to the prestigious Fortune Global list (the list of the top ranking companies, released by CNN Money on an annual basis), 65% have a presence on Twitter, 50% have video channels on YouTube, 54% have fan pages on Facebook and 33% have regularly updated blogs.'

This book is aimed at helping business owners realise what social media can help them accomplish. If you are planning to use it for your business, this book will guide you in the right direction. In case you already have social media practices in place, you can significantly improve their effectiveness while evaluating the other options that can work for you.

This book will tell you everything you need to know about aligning social media with your business needs. Perhaps, one of the most useful aspects is that it features an entire chapter on what you can do to attract relevant traffic and to ensure conversions.

The book has individual user manuals which allow business users to evaluate the options that are available to them. Also, the pros and cons of the major social media websites are outlined briefly. Last but not least, the book has a chapter where you will come across answers to the most frequently asked questions. This book is full of useful tips to transform your current business into an effective, successful, money-making machine. It is time you outpaced all the competition, it is time you started reading.

Chapter One

What is Social Media?

History of social media

Social media is an essential part of not just our lives but our society as well. Social media was once limited to only those with an in-depth understanding of computers. However, today it is available for anyone and everyone and has expanded to the extent that we find it difficult to imagine our lives without it. Let's take a look at how it all started.

Since the very beginning, social media has revolved around two ideas – gathering information and socialising. Using this concept, the Bulletin Board Systems, or BBSs, were introduced in February 1978. They allowed access to only a single user at a time and they were, in fact, the first type of websites that allowed users to interact with each other but, of course, in a slower fashion.

In 1994, GeoCities, a personal home page service was initiated. It was made available to the general public in 1998 and was purchased by Yahoo! for 3.57 billion in the year 1999. GeoCities closed down in 2009. In the year 1997, the first ever social media service, the renowned SixDegrees.com came into the picture. It earned great popularity. At the peak of its popularity, the service claimed to have around a million users.

In August 1999, the blogging service Blogger was launched. Google purchased Blogger in 2003. In 2002, the website Friendster.com emerged on the web landscape. An unbelievable increase was observed in the number of the site's users in 2008. However, its reputation soon started to fade. In May 2003, LinkedIn surfaced as a one-of-a-kind website giving birth to the concept of corporate social networking.

'Since the very beginning, social media has revolved around two ideas – gathering information and socialising.'

In July 2003, MySpace started gaining popularity. The website was acquired by News Corp in 2005 for a price of $580 million. The website was known to receive about 75 million visitors each month till the end of 2008.

On the 4th of February, 2004, the phenomenal social networking site Facebook was born. Initially, it could be used by the students of Harvard University only. However, it expanded soon and was opened to 800 colleges across the country within a year. By the month of September 2006, Facebook was accessible to anyone aged 13 and beyond. In December, 2006, Yahoo! tried to purchase Facebook by making an offer of $1 billion. This offer was ultimately refused by Facebook.

In March 2006, Twitter was launched. Being an unconventional social media service, it allows its users to interact via 'tweets' where each tweet can have as many as 140 characters.

In April 2008, Facebook accomplished a milestone as its popularity outshone that of MySpace in terms of the number of unique visitors it received in a month. On the 2nd December, 2009, the number of Facebook members reached 350 million. This number continued to rise as it reached 400 million in February 2010.

On 28th June 2011, Google+ introduced its beta version in the market. In less than two weeks, ten million people around the world joined it with the number of items shared each day estimated to be one billion. LinkedIn became the second most popular website in the US with 33.9 million users on July 8th 2011, with MySpace following closely behind with its 33.5 million users.

On the 13th July 2011, Twitter celebrated its 5th birthday and according to resources, the giant is known to deliver approximately 350 million tweets each day.

At the time of writing, Twitter and Facebook boast of having 140 million and a billion members respectively. As the number of social networking sites launched keeps on increasing, it leaves no doubt that we are living in the social media age.

Social media is, indeed, crucial to our existence despite the fact that it has not been around for long. In less than a decade, it has touched millions of lives and has changed the way we interact with friends, read news or share

'On November 30th, 2010, Facebook's value was estimated to be $50 billion. Just after five months of reaching the $400 billion target in February, Facebook got half a million more users.'

8

interests. The technology has connected the world in a way that was never even imagined before. With social media, the world is a smaller place and its inhabitants more closely knit than ever before.

There are countless individuals who are now using social media and so it comes as no surprise that business owners see social media as a promising platform to market their services and products. Those who are not yet involved in social media have no idea what they are missing. Don't be the odd one out. There is an exciting world of opportunities so why wait?

Impact on society

Welcome to the social media revolution. Today, whether you choose to embrace or reject the technology, one thing is for sure, there is no way social media can be ignored. There is a reason social media websites such as Facebook, Twitter, Pinterest and Google+ have not only grown tremendously in very little time but have also acquired reputations others cannot dream of.

When it comes to the impact of social media on society, let's take a look at some fascinating statistics:

- Blogging and social networking sites account for a total of 22% of all time spent on the Internet.

- Twitter played such an influential role in the Iranian elections conducted in 2009, that the State Department of US requested Twitter to delay a network upgrade that was scheduled to take place in the busy hours of the day. Twitter complied and postponed the downtime to the early hours of morning.

- A day before the US presidential elections in 2008 were to be conducted, the candidate representing the Republican party, John McCain, had 620,359 Facebook supporters as compared to Democratic candidate Barrack Obama's 2,379,102 supporters.

- According to resources, 60 million individuals claimed to have received help with major issues through social media websites in 2010. According to them, these websites helped them connect to experts and friends who assisted them in making well-informed decisions.

- 59% of all students reported that they used social media sites as a platform to discuss careers, assignments and college planning.

- Parents expressed their gratitude for social media as they believe it has facilitated learning and has allowed children to communicate more clearly and effectively.

- Acquiring health-related information is the third most popular activity on the Internet and social media sites have played a significant role in the reduction of several dangerous health conditions, with the most notable being memory retention and stroke recovery.

'Social media is neither good nor bad, it is not useful nor useless, evil or a godsend. At the end of the day, it comes down to how you use it.'

These statistics suggest that social media impacts our society influentially. People are turning to social media sites for all sorts of reasons, from getting quick answers to queries, to finding location-based data easily. We are relying on social media heavily. For instance, when it comes to making purchases, instead of getting something right away, we now prefer to read reviews and to seek input or approval of bloggers.

Social media has started an era where it is not only a tool to improve communications but aims to improve our wellbeing as well. However, what cannot be emphasised enough is its use in moderation. Social media is neither good nor bad, it is not useful nor useless, evil or a godsend. At the end of the day, it comes down to how you use it. With the appropriate checks and balances in place, one can say that social media has empowered the common man to go beyond his means to make smarter decisions in every single area of his life.

Impact on businesses

Social media is fun. It may have served as a platform for better communication at the very start, but people soon realised that it can help bring their business several benefits. When used competently, it can help any business secure an edge above all others. The impact of social media on business is, undoubtedly, enormous.

An increasing number of Internet users now prefer to shop online. In addition, 70% of online shoppers trust consumer opinion they find on the Internet. Blogs and social media networks continue to top the charts as the most visited among all websites. These statistics show that businesses, regardless of their size, are finding it fruitful to join the social media trend and build their plan of action around the most valuable and effective practices.

Unlike traditional business tactics which suggests that business and pleasure do not mix, social media has radically changed that idea and the way business is done. Now there is a focus on entertainment and engagement. While the ways in which social media influence businesses are virtually countless, a handful of the most notable ones are listed below:

Social media – A synonym for 'word of mouth marketing'

Businesses have relied on 'word of mouth marketing' for years. We are living in an age where we are doing some online research before we head out to make even the most insignificant of purchases. We look for some kind of recommendation in the form of feedback, comments or reviews. In this way social media closely resembles what 'word-of-mouth' was once believed to accomplish but in a more time-effective manner.

This tactic encourages users to express their opinion of your brand, product, or service. Social media helps customers evaluate if your business is reputable and if it can be trusted. This helps generate leads and eases the conversion of visitors into customers. In short, you get to build brand recognition while securing maximum exposure for your business.

Your target market is using it

Most of the individuals today use one kind of social media site or the other. These sites are the most visited ones among all and whether the reason for usage is acquiring information, shopping or games, social media has allowed people to easily locate and reach whatever it is they are looking for.

Quadruples your visibility

One of the most attractive features of social media is that it is one of the most practical means to connect to your target market. Using resources like LinkedIn groups and Twitter hashtags, it is possible to reach your client base

'Unlike traditional business tactics which suggests that business and pleasure do not mix, social media has radically changed that idea and the way business is done.'

and engage them into conversations. Also, you can spread up-to-date content by syndicating it to multiple channels. This translates into more relevant traffic which means better chances to improve sales.

Achieves competitive advantage

Perhaps one thing that earns social media an edge above all the other marketing tactics is the two-way communication it establishes. Instead of just allowing businesses to promote their offerings, social media has given audiences a forum to connect with other buyers and your business. Social media is a tool that can help you determine how people perceive your business. Furthermore, by using industry keywords, you can stay abreast of any conversations surrounding your competitors or brand.

'Perhaps one thing that earns social media an edge above all the other marketing tactics is the two-way communication it establishes.'

Provides value

Social media empowers businesses. It gives them the ability to engage their potential prospects with informative and interesting content such as tweets, posts and blogs. When you help customers with any of their needs, they will sing praises for you that have no end. Provide valuable content free and get lots of recommendations in return.

Humanise your company

Customers like to voice their opinions. The ability to leave feedback gives them the satisfaction that their opinions matter. Although conventionally businesses use logos and symbols to represent themselves, often we come across people who want to buy from a certain buyer just because they know them personally. This is what social media helps you achieve. Social media gives businesses a more human feel. Only by putting up a face, name or relationship, any business can go a long way.

Search engines base their results on social media

Social media can help improve your search engine rankings. Wondering how? When several people share your content, your blogs or refer to your website, it means they found it entertaining, informative or useful. When that happens, search engines realise that you have something valuable to offer. The search engine pays attention to your website and this ultimately leads to better search engine rankings.

Amazing customer service

One of the key benefits of social media is that it allows businesses to improve customer service. While this aspect has been discussed in detail in the next section, one can briefly state that social media has provided a less formal platform where customers can express their approval or disappointment in the form of feedback, reviews or comments.

Businesses have to realise how social media can spell success for them. It is one of the most useful marketing tools available at this time. Mastering social media practices can be extremely beneficial because of the assortment of possibilities they bring. Remember, social media for businesses is vital as it could be the difference between losing credibility and staying one step ahead of your competition.

'One of the key benefits of social media is that it allows businesses to improve customer service.'

How social media has improved customer service

Managing relationships is not about having a customer directory with telephone numbers, email or residential addresses. There is more to it than meets the eye. While at one hand, social media has offered some remarkable benefits for businesses, on the other, it has played its role in shifting power from companies to clients.

A single wrong step you take can bring your prestigious brand down on its knees. Social media has been recognised as a great tool, one that was quickly taken on board by enterprises across the globe because of better customer service you can provide through it.

Improved customer service is one of the principle advantages that social media can secure for any business. It brings about a one-of-a-kind opportunity to build up stronger relationships between a company and its valuable clientele.

By making use of social media, a business can guarantee real-time connections with existing customers as well as with potential prospects. It gives businesses a chance to convey and promote a positive brand image. The higher the degree and frequency of engagement a business secures, the stronger the company-customer relationships and the greater the sales.

Who's using it?

While you may find it hard to believe, the most well-known brands, the likes of Dell, AT&T, Apple, Coca-Cola and Nike are making use of social media. Why? Because they know that they can benefit from positive word of mouth. They know that any news (positive or negative) will be exponentially broadcast across multiple social media channels such as Twitter, Facebook, etc. By fitting social media into their marketing practices, these companies have not only earned customer satisfaction and growth in sales, but have also gained product reputation as well.

Customers love social media

Those who have made use of telephonic customer service even once are of the opinion that it is quite annoying pressing one button after the other only to wait for your call to be transferred to someone else.

Customer service provided through email is even more disappointing. It takes weeks for a single email to be answered. This is where social media scores. It is instant. It is hassle free and since companies know that good news travels fast but bad news travels faster, they respond within minutes which ultimately translates into customer satisfaction.

How is it done?

- Monitor – Social media allows businesses to see who is talking about them. Whether it is for better or for worse, there is countless software out there that will give you a complete picture of the popularity of your brand among the masses and classes. For instance, if you find a customer complaining to his/her friend about one of your products, you can jump in and resolve the issue then and there. This will make customers feel valued.

- Engage – Interaction with customers does not necessarily have to be about solving some problem. Instead, it can be solely used to achieve a certain level of engagement. By monitoring a particular customer who is promoting your brand, you can easily elevate his/her experience by sending discount coupons, thank you gifts or free products. With social media, you can stay more up to date about how your customers feel about you.

- Public attention – What makes social media the most powerful means to stay connected with customers is the transparency it suggests. If a customer is showing their disappointment publicly, it can be addressed publicly as well. Just show that you are sorry about the problem and take corrective measures immediately. This effort will go a long way because you will be giving off the signal that your company goes to any lengths to keep their customers happy.

Unleash the full potential of social media and improve customer service through it. The technology offers incredible opportunities of having a contented clientele. Turn those frowns upside down and make the most of social media to keep things that way.

'Social media allows businesses to see who is talking about them.'

Expansion of social media – Smartphones

Smartphones are gadgets that have allowed those on the go to stay connected to their professional and personal lives. The gadget has bridged the gap that once existed between mobile phones and computers. This is because, today, a smartphone is capable of doing everything that could only be done on a computer previously.

From checking emails to browsing websites, multimedia production to using amazing apps, the smartphone is capable of it all. In fact, it is the competency of these gadgets that has triggered the growth of social media popularity.

Smartphones have come a long way since their introduction in the market. With the number of those buying smartphones constantly increasing, a surge has been observed in the fame of social media sites as well. There are several apps for smartphones now that can allow you to organise and manage your social media account and to view information over a phone. In 2011, a survey conducted revealed that 84% of smartphone owners in the UK used their gadgets to look up local information. Out of these, 80% made a purchase through social media sites.

In addition, according to a report released by comScore, it was found as compared to PCs or laptops, individuals spend a considerably larger portion of their time using social networks on smartphones.

Today, most smartphones feature dedicated keys for popular social networking websites. Publishing constant updates about your personal and professional life is now a common trend among the young and old alike. Especially for those on the go, this comes as a definite plus.

What has further led to the expansion of social media is that smartphones establish ease of use that was never known before. Faster Internet service enables a smartphone owner to keep track of all the current happenings in their circle with social media right on their fingertips. Thus, one can say that the emergence of smartphones has served as a support system for the boom of the social media trend.

'30% of smartphone users in the UK used it to make purchases in 2011. 22% of smartphone owners take their smartphones shopping intentionally to compare prices and get product information.'

The way forward

Social media has provided an opening for businesses. It has initiated a change movement. A few years ago, enterprises were sceptical about having a web presence. While some were viewing it as a technical challenge, others perceived it as a change in the way business is done.

Today, businesses that have failed to keep up with the ever-changing times are the ones to have suffered the most. Their resistance to change has doomed them to failure because what they did not foresee that consumer habits are changing.

Social media users are phenomenally growing in numbers. It is apparent that consumers are smarter than ever before. They are communicating with each other to seek advice or information before making any sort of purchasing decisions.

Technology has provided the means. Now the responsibility lies with businesses to bring about a competitive change. It is high time for business entities to let go of the same old conventional practices and to move ahead with social media as the strongest weapon in their arsenal against competition.

Social media is vital for businesses to carve their way forward. There is a dire need for business owners to change their mindset. Using traditional marketing strategies is no longer going to pay off. Social media is the new business approach, with relationship and content development being its principal aspects.

'Social media is vital for businesses to carve their way forward.'

To succeed, businesses have to achieve a deeper understanding of their target market, find out where it resides and interact with it effectively. They need to provide information interesting enough to encourage customers into further interacting with them and eventually nurture long-lasting relationships. Surge forward with social media or your competitor will.

Summing Up

- From its conception, the two basic ideas of social media are gathering information and socialising.

- The earliest form of social media was introduced in February 1978, using a concept called the Bulletin Board System (BBS). These websites were the first of their kind to allow users to interact with each other.

- Today, Facebook is the most popular social networking site, boasting over a billion users worldwide.

- Businesses view social media as a lucrative platform to market their services and products.

- Social media is accessed for a multitude of reasons, including socialising, research, help and advice related to both health and business as well as various other subjects, purchasing goods and services, marketing, etc.

- The introduction of gadgets such as smartphones to the market has seen a huge expansion in the use and popularity of social media.

Chapter Two

Different Type of Social Media Tools

The first step is finding out about social media options that can work wonders for you. Aligning social media with your business objectives should be viewed as a project and, as with every project, a prerequisite is to find out what tools are needed and an understanding of how they can be used.

Social media provides a variety of tools for businesses. Only by determining what is available, social media can help an enterprise achieve its designated milestones. Without proper knowledge of the tools that are to be used for any project, it is natural for even the smartest social marketer to get confused.

The varieties of social media tools that are available are quite overwhelming. Describing these tools in great detail will be an enormous undertaking. However, briefly explaining the types of social media tools that a business can use is a more realistic approach.

The core objective social media intends to fulfil is conversation and engagement. In return, the strategies are expected to render results which could be anything from greater customer satisfaction to improved sales. Here it is also important to understand that the services or products a company sells also have an influence on the social media tools a company can use. Read on and think of out-of-the-box ways to leverage the following tools for your company.

By the end of this chapter, you'll not only be able to categorise social media tools into types but will also have a good grasp over what differentiates one from the other.

Social networks

Social networks are probably the most popular of all tools. Opening multiple new and unconventional channels for communication with customers, social networks are allowing enterprises to converse with new and existing customers on a more personal level.

In essence, social networks are meant to facilitate interaction between groups of people on common ground. This can be people sharing common interests, backgrounds, activities or connections in real life. Often, a social network service allows an individual to represent himself through a profile. Here one can manage and organise his/her social links and the additional services provided vary from one network to another.

The growth and popularity of social networks is no secret. Every other day, some service is making a new record for receiving the highest number of unique users over a period of time, surpassing the popularity of all others. In any case, social networks are indeed the ideal place to connect to your future prospects and to keep the current ones engaged.

Among all, Facebook and LinkedIn are the most famous social networks. Founded in 2004 by Mark Zuckerberg, Facebook is presently the largest social media network in the world, with over 1 billion users across the globe as of September 2012. This utility has not only taken businesses to the heights of success but has also spelled out a new and unique way of conducting business for them.

On the other hand, LinkedIn is more of a corporate social network mainly used for professional networking. Introduced in December 2002, the service has 175 million users across the globe recorded in 2012, and is used in over 200 countries. LinkedIn enables users to manage their professional identity and to engage with those in their professional network. It provides a chance to access insights and knowledge as well as career opportunities.

'Opening multiple new and unconventional channels for communication with customers, social networks are allowing enterprises to converse with new and existing customers on a more personal level.'

Blogs

Blogs are easily the most useful tools for businesses to achieve dialogue with customers and to promote conversions. Blogs help to create a trusted environment between a business and its clientele.

There is a wide array of available blogging tools that come with comprehensive templates. Using them, any individual or business owner can start publishing content right away. Some of the most famous blogging sites are WordPress, Blogger and LiveJournal.

WordPress is actually software that comes with all the tools essential for the development of an attractive blog or website. The service highlights the maintenance of high web standards, usability rules and aesthetics. WordPress, unlike others, also offers a version that is self-hosted. This ensures greater flexibility and makes WordPress the principal choice for business-based blogging.

Blogger is also a blog-publishing service. It allows the creation of private blogs that can be accessed by multiple users at a time. Launched in 1999, it was bought by Google in 2003 and using this service, users can publish their blogs on multiple hosts.

LiveJournal is also a notable blog-publishing platform where users with similar interests or passions can communicate with each other. In other words, here users can maintain a journal, diary or blog. It started in April 1999 and is still the preferred choice of several bloggers.

Wikis

Everyone that's an avid Internet user knows about wikis. After search engines, they are the first choice when any kind of information is needed. A wiki is a website developed by contributors from across the globe that provides detailed information on any given topic. These pages can easily be edited or modified by anyone. Most of the contributors write on content which is either community based or on specific topics or interests. Wiki has become a great source of information for individuals from around the globe to research about a variety of different interests, geographical locations, history, individuals or businesses.

Wikis are actually applications that are web based. Users are allowed to create, modify and distribute content on topics of their choice. Wiki websites are supported by intelligent software and all the changes in the content are achieved through a browser.

'Some of the most famous blogging sites are WordPress, Blogger and LiveJournal.'

When the use of wikis for businesses is in question, it can come in handy to know that enterprises across the globe are now using them to their advantage. Enterprises are finding wikis a safe bet for providing low-cost employee training. Also, wikis are being used to facilitate the process of product development. Wikis are also used for communicating business-related information to the concerned parties.

While there are many stand-alone wikis that have been developed, they are usually developed collaboratively. Wikis serve a variety of purposes such as note taking and central knowledge management. They can be intranet as well as community websites that come with unique features. For instance, it is possible to define different levels of security to limit access to content. The most famous wikis used today are Wikipedia, BizWiki, and Investopedia.

'Wikis serve a variety of purposes such as note taking and central knowledge management. They can be intranet as well as community websites that come with unique features.'

Wikipedia

Wikipedia is a free encyclopaedia that anyone can edit. Offered in multiple languages, it boasts of having 4,088,425 articles in English language only. The website is operated by Wikimedia Foundation and is famous for instantly routing users to pages where they can find detailed information on any topic they are looking for.

BizWiki

BizWiki, on the other hand, is a free and well-maintained directory of enterprises or businesses. Anyone can contribute to it and make changes. The network is aimed at becoming the most comprehensive and largest of all American business directories on the Web. It is the biggest collection of resources to help researchers find relevant information on topics or projects. Links to databases, reference books, websites and a variety of other sources of authentic information can be found here. Searches related to any topic can be initiated using keywords.

Investopedia

Investopedia, unlike all others, is the largest resource aimed at educating people about finance and investments. Founded by Cory Wagner and Cory Janssen in 1999, this website is one of the most celebrated sources for acquiring finance-related information. The popularity of the website is evident from the fact that it was acquired by the famous US-based publishing company Forbes in 2007. Today, it is operated by ValueClick, an online advertising company, which purchased it from Forbes for $43 million.

Podcasts

Those who want their business to be heard don't need to look any further. With tools like podcast, businesses can communicate their message more efficiently and effectively than ever before. A podcast is not text or photograph, instead it is a personal recording that includes your business message. You can make this recording on your personal computer and upload it on your server.

Now, interested parties can come to your server, download your recording and listen to it whenever and wherever they want. Using verbal communications to influence individuals is nothing new and this is what podcasts are all about.

With the prevalent use of iPods and other devices supporting digital media storage, social media has given audiences the ability to take any message along with them. They can then listen to it, say while going somewhere in a car or out for an evening walk. Podcasts have not only established convenience for users but have also spanned several opportunities for any business as well.

Apple's flagship store, iTunes, is the most eminent resource of podcasts. Here any and every individual can launch a free podcast spree with thousands of podcasts right at one's fingertips. iTunes allows you to search for podcasts on the basis of popularity. Businesses can take advantage of this service by browsing through the most popular podcast searches to determine the title for their podcast. Also, iTunes allows users to see which podcast is topping the charts to determine how well their business message is getting across.

Content sharing websites

Content sharing websites, as the name implies, are those that allow users to share content whether it is in the form of photo, audio or video. What actually happens is that users can submit the content and can share it with anyone residing anywhere in the world. Whether it is a home video of your kids playing or that of a party you hosted at your home, sharing content with those in your circle has now become extremely easy.

While photo and audio sharing are also well-loved online activities, it is actually video sharing that gets marketers excited. Some of the most popular content sharing sites are YouTube, Flickr and Digg.

'Content sharing for businesses cannot be stressed enough. It can be an incredible opportunity for enterprises to create brand awareness and secure global reach. With any other marketing means, you can target only a specific community or group of individuals. However, as far as content sharing websites are concerned, they have breathed life into the idea of every single business going global. It is no longer just about your town, your state or your country. It is about engaging people and transforming them into customers regardless of how far they are physically separated from you.

'Content sharing for businesses cannot be stressed enough. It can be an incredible opportunity for enterprises to create brand awareness and secure global reach.'

YouTube

YouTube is primarily a website that is aimed at sharing videos not just with your friends or family, but with the world. Introduced in February 2005, YouTube is now a subsidiary of Google Inc. If you are wondering what it can do for your business, you might be surprised to know that Justin Bieber, the young artist to have taken the music world by storm, became as famous as he is today because of YouTube. His mom uploaded some videos of his performances at local events. Scooter Braun, a talent manager from Atlanta, saw these videos and realised Justin's potential. Justin was then introduced to Usher, the R'n'B superstar and since then has not looked back. If YouTube can do this for an artist, imagine how meteorically it can help your business rise.

Flickr

Flickr is a video hosting and image hosting website that was launched in 2004. Soon acquired by Yahoo!, Flickr was developed with two basic goals in mind: to allow people to share their photos with people who matter, and to introduce an innovative method of organising and managing videos and photos. Home to more than five billion photos, the website allows its users to dive into a world of photos where creativity and beauty knows no bounds.

Digg

Digg is the name if you want to stay up to date with everything happening in your surroundings. Digg actually provides insight on the most sought-after and talked-about pictures, videos and stores on the Web. Users have the ability to vote content up or down. In a nutshell, this website tells you what Internet users are talking about right now.

Microblogging

Microblogging is quite similar to blogging. However, unlike traditional blogging where there is no limit to word count, microblogging is concise. Its content is significantly shorter in terms of size and allows users to exchange smaller elements of content in the form of images, links or text. These smaller content elements are then referred to as 'micro posts'.

As is the case with traditional blogging, users can post about a wide array of topics ranging from general (what a user is doing at that particular moment) to specifics (such as household maintenance or sports cars). Microblogs serving commercial purposes also exist. These are meant to market websites, products, services or any collaborations formed within an organisation. Different microblogging websites offer different features which can range from privacy settings to using alternate ways for publishing entries. These microblogs can then include digital video, digital audio, email, instant or text messaging. The most famous microblogging websites where a business can interact and converse with its prospects to develop closer networking bonds are Twitter, Facebook and Pownce.

The previously mentioned networks are smart social media solutions. When their portability is combined with the ease provided by mobile devices, this seemingly simple approach can be a lifesaver for any business.

Enterprises can use microblogging for the formation of online communities on the basis of common friendships, interests or associations. Business owners can create a positive brand image with a following of microbloggers that are interested in their offerings.

Twitter

Twitter is the most popular of all microblogging networks. Twitter makes it possible for its users to read and send messages of a maximum of 140 characters. These messages are known as 'tweets'. Founded on March 21st 2006, Twitter boasts of being one of the 10 most visited websites on the Internet.

Facebook

Facebook is essentially a social networking service that has employed microblogging as one of its features. Here users can share any of the happenings in their life by posting them in the form of status updates. However, what makes it different from Twitter is that Facebook does not limit users to the number of characters that can be used. Available in 70 languages, Facebook receives the highest number of unique visitors each month after Google.

Online forums

Internet forums, or online forums, are fundamentally a type of website where online discussions can be initiated. These conversations are held in the form of messages that participants post from across the globe. Forums have specific jargon, for instance a single conversation is referred to as a 'thread'.

Online forums are a practical approach that enterprises can use to engage prospects into conversations related to specific topics of interest. Businesses particularly find them useful as they help develop a close-knit community of trusted individuals.

While there are different ways online forums can benefit a business, one of the most significant is that they can be used to provide instant service and support. It allows businesses to gain insight into consumer patterns and to secure a wider client base. Several businesses have made use of online forums in the past and have successfully met their expectations.

Instant messaging

IM, or instant messaging, is a casual way of communicating over the Web. Instant messaging is all about the exchange of text-based messages between a receiver and sender. Since it is an exchange of dialogue in real time, the idea was to strengthen connections between users. Instant messaging is believed to fall under the category of online chat and using it, individuals can interact in a multi-user environment.

Instant messaging soon earned popularity in the business arena as well. What was once considered a plaything for consumers soon became a tool that assisted businesses to achieve rapid communication with their clientele. It is flexible, it is instantaneous, and it works anywhere and everywhere.

The most eminent examples of instant messaging are chat rooms, Window's Live Messenger and Skype. Chat rooms are not just about online chats conducted in real time, they actually provide graphical environments for individuals to interact.

Windows Live Messenger, previously known as MSN Messenger, is an instant messaging service that was developed and released by Microsoft 13 years ago. The service supports a variety of platforms, and statistics revealed that a few years back, it received traffic as high as 330 million users every month.

Skype is also instant messaging software. It was released in August 2003 and it now is a product of the Microsoft Corporation which acquired it for $8.5 billion. In 2010, the service had 600 million registered users which is a

'While there are different ways online forums can benefit a business, one of the most significant is that they can be used to provide instant service and support.'

phenomenal success. Apart from instant messaging, Skype allows users to communicate through audio and video using a microphone and webcam respectively.

Social media dashboards

Last but not the least, a popular tool many businesses are using to effectively manage their web presence is social media dashboard. Offering several perks to businesses, dashboards allow information to be managed and organised in a way that it can be easily read and understood.

Every business relies on more than one channel to manage their web existence. A business can be posting regular tweets on Twitter, updating statuses on Facebook, or uploading podcasts to a server. Doing all this is just not enough. A business needs to determine how the audience is responding to its efforts. This is the beauty of social media dashboards. They help you to accomplish just that. Dashboards provide a unified platform where you can integrate data from a wealth of resources and see measurable results.

'Dashboards provide a unified platform where you can integrate data from a wealth of resources and see measurable results.'

When it comes to social media dashboards, there are many choices available on the market. However, the one dashboard that a lot of enterprises have found reliable is HootSuite.

HootSuite

HootSuite is a management system for social media with brand management the primary objective it was created to achieve. The founder, Ryan Holmes, introduced it in 2008. It allows its users to integrate the most popular social networking websites including Google+, LinkedIn, FourSquare, MySpace, Twitter, Facebook and many others.

HootSuite also has an app directory to provide support for social media websites such as Flickr, YouTube, Digg, Tumblr, etc. According to recent statistics, by January 2012, the dashboard claimed to have more than 3 million users who were measuring how well their marketing efforts were paying off.

Summing Up

- Social media tools fall into several different categories, each with their own purpose and facilities.

- Facebook and LinkedIn are two of the most famous social networks. Used by people wanting to 'share' profiles, experiences, common interests, etc.; Facebook is widely used on a more social level, but businesses still utilise its huge popularity to amazing success, whilst LinkedIn is more a corporate networking site.

- Blogs are the most useful tool for businesses to interact with customers and promote their services, whilst also receiving valuable consumer feedback. Microblogging is a concise form of blogging, with Twitter being the most influential and popular site, publishing around 350 million tweets every day.

- Second only to search engines, wikis are accessed to find out information and conduct research. Businesses use wikis to aid employee training, product development and communication of business-related information. The most famous wikis used today are Wikipedia, BizWiki and Investopedia.

- Podcasts allow personal recordings and business messages to be downloaded and listened to. Currently, Apple's iTunes is the most established source of podcasts.

- Content sharing websites allow users to share photos, vieos, etc. and has prompted the introduction of popular sites such as YouTube and Flickr.

- Online forums are fundamentally online discussions or conversations that are held in the form of messages posted from around the world. They are useful to businesses as they allow them insight into consumer patterns and enable them to provide instant service and support.

- IM (instant messaging) is an exchange of dialogue over the Web held in real time. Some of the most popular IM sites are Windows Live Messenger and Skype, plus chat rooms.

- Social media dashboards allow information to be managed and communicated effectively, with the most popular being HootSuite.

Chapter Three

Choosing the Right Social Media for Your Business Needs

By now you must have realised that social media is just what you need to get the wheels going in the right direction for your business. All you need is relevant information to share, a client base that is interested in your products or offerings and sufficient resources to devise a social media strategy that can work for you.

Amid all the hype surrounding social media, what cannot be overlooked is the vitality of doing it right. When portraying to the world a positive image of your business, if things do not go as planned, you can easily end up damaging your reputation and relationship with customers.

As a business owner, you must have a good idea of how referrals can serve as a stimulus for business growth. If not the strongest, referrals are indeed one of the most powerful means to generate business. In the same way, social media also serves as an extension of referrals, a means to expand business.

Have you ever wondered why customers prefer a particular brand, service or product over others? Because customers have found exactly what they have been looking for. It has been delivered to them just the way they wanted.

Enterprises that have excelled financially are those that have successfully inspired customer satisfaction for those dealing with them. Same is the case with social media. A business has to ensure that the customer's needs are met and delivered in the desired fashion.

'Social media also serves as an extension of referrals, a means to expand business.

With the availability of a variety of social media tools today, one may be at a loss as to what to choose.

People should realise that social media tools are not all equal. One should not be expected to deliver results the same as others, as the choice of social media channels is entirely subjective to the nature of your business. Several different social media tools can be used together, but using them all is not good practice. It will lead you nowhere as managing information on multiple platforms will become an exceedingly difficult task. As a result, any efforts to promote your business will backfire.

This chapter will shed light on how businesses can evolve using social media. We will also discuss the role technology plays in strengthening relationships between businesses and customers that earns them the commercial advantage. We will also talk about the specifications of famous social media sites that every business owner must know before making a leap. At the end of this chapter we will outline important dos and don'ts when using social media for business. In the following chapter you will identify any social media-related risks and the strategies that an enterprise can use to stay in the game. The reach of the famous social media platforms and the audience you can target through them have also been outlined. So, keep reading.

'Social media is a channel with several breakthroughs waiting for you at the other end.'

Social media websites – Specifications

Maintaining an effective web presence is easier said than done. You just don't wake up one morning, decide you want to join the social media league, snap your fingers and it's done. Social media is a channel with several breakthroughs waiting for you at the other end.

People may not see the advertisements printed in newspapers, pasted on billboards or broadcast on television, but an offer on Facebook's News Feed or in a tweet is more likely to catch their eyes.

A business's web presence takes a lot of factors into consideration. There is a lot of effort put into it. Since social media is used as a means to market a brand, a lot is at stake, and taking any risks will not be a practical undertaking. It is of paramount importance that you have all the ingredients in just the right proportions. The profile images should be attractive, the descriptions should be engaging, and the character counts should maintain interest, not to forget taglines that come in all shapes and sizes.

In an attempt to make things easier and to save you the inconvenience of seeking various sources of knowledge, we have put together a list of specifications for the most common social networking websites. This will give you a fair idea of the aspects you need to take into account before narrowing down your options for social media tools.

Facebook specifications

Specifications for the timeline page on Facebook are as follows:

Content Bandwidth	850 Pixels
Banner Image	850 x 315 Pixels
Avatar Image	125 x 125 Pixels
Avatar Icon	50 x 50 Pixels
Width of Image Content	400 Pixels
Width of Link Thumbnail	90 Pixels

Specifications for the brand page on Facebook timeline are as follows:

Content Bandwidth	850 Pixels
Banner Image	850 x 315 Pixels
Avatar Image	125 x 125 Pixels
Avatar Icon	50 x 50 Pixels
Width of Image Content	400 Pixels
Width of Link Thumbnail	90 Pixels

Other image rules that Facebook has imposed for a business's cover images are listed below:

- Cover image cannot include purchase-related or price-related information such as 'download by logging on to our website' or 'get a 40% discount'.

- The cover image should not contain any contact information such as a web address, email address or any other information that is usually part of a business's 'About Us' section.

- There should not be a reference to any elements of user interface, for instance share, like or any other features.

- There should not be any calls to action such as 'purchase now' or 'tell a friend'.

Twitter specifications

Specifications for Twitter are as follows:

Content Width	920 Pixels (Centre)
Header Image	1200 x 600 Pixels (5MB Max.)
Background Image	Maximum 800 Kb
Position for Background Image	Left Aligned
Large Display of Avatar Icon	128 x 128 Pixels
Small Display of Avatar Image	48 x 48 Pixels
Thumbnail Display of Image (Right)	83 x 83 Pixels
Thumbnail Display of Image (Gallery)	150 x 150 Pixels
Name Limit	20 Characters
Bio Limit	160 Characters
Tweet Limit	140 Characters

YouTube specifications

Specifications for YouTube are as follows:

Content Width	960 Pixels (Centre)
Background Image	Maximum 1760 Pixels
Position of Background Image	Centre
Large Display of Avatar Icon	88 x 88 Pixels
Small Display of Avatar Icon	36 x 36 Pixels

Google+ specifications

Specifications for Google+ are as follows:

Content Width	500 Pixels
Banner Image for Profile	890 x 180 Pixels
Macro Disply of Profile Image	32 x 32 Pixels
Small Display of Profile Image	48 x 48 Pixels
Large Display of Profile Image	250 x 250 Pixels
Maximum Width of Inline Image	401 Pixels
Maximum Width of Thumbnail Image	160 Pixels
Maximum Height of Thumbnail Image	120 Pixels

LinkedIn specifications

Specifications for Twitter are as follows:

Content Width	160 x 600 Pixels
Animation Limit	30 Seconds
Background Image	40 Kb Maximum
Text Link Dimensions	960 x 70 Pixels
Text Limit	90 Characters

Dos and don'ts of social media

'Social media can offer all the exposure you can ask for and is a phenomenal platform to get the best out of your efforts without making large investments.'

You may be a smart social media marketer knowing all the angles or you may be a newbie panicking at every single negative comment. In either case, you are in the thick of it and you have to boost your web presence by hook or by crook.

Social media can offer all the exposure you can ask for and is a phenomenal platform to get the best out of your efforts without making large investments, but it works both way. One wrong step and you are in hot water.

This section aims to take a quick look at what you should and shouldn't do when it comes to social media for business. With all the suggestions listed, it will be easier for you to dodge all those challenges competitors may hurl your way.

Dos

- Do know your audience – You should know what people need and address it in the best possible manner. What are the conversations they are having? Is their response satisfactory? Are they happy with you? What is the kind of content they prefer on different channels?

- Do promote your pages on multiple platforms – Often efforts to create buzz backfire because business owners do not understand that it's not possible to reach people if they don't know you exist. Use every possible medium to announce your presence. Asking existing customers or regular shoppers to follow you on Twitter or 'like' your Facebook page is easier than you can think.

- Do respond to feedback – If your customer is spending his/her time to express their opinion about your products or services, don't forget to respond to them at once. Efficiency in this area will be appreciated by customers and you will indirectly communicate it to customers that every single one of them is important to you and your brand.

- Do respect content ownership – Don't steal anything. Not only it is unethical, you can get into trouble if found out by the owner. Even if you are sharing a useful article, don't forget to credit the author.

- Do interact with competitors – It is perfectly fine to follow your competitors and see what they are doing. Similarly, allow them to look at your approaches. Be careful not to attack them. It is disrespectful and you will be casting a negative impression of your brand on others.

Don'ts

Now we'll take a quick look at don'ts that have to be avoided by all means.

- Do not set and forget – A mistake common to most businesses is viewing social media as a one-time strategy. It is essentially a process that goes on and on where you can win only by branding consistently.

- Don't be 'sales pitchy' – Social media does help generate sales but believing that it serves no other purpose is wrong. Social media is meant to create a community of individuals interested in your brand. If you are effortlessly creating content that people like, they will themselves share it with others to help you grow.

- Don't ignore negative feedback – If you are behaving as if negative content doesn't exist, it will give the signal that you are least bothered about how your customers feel and how to rectify their disapproval or disappointment. Be ultra responsive to negative comments and show that you care about user experiences.

- Don't blow your own trumpet – Don't overly highlight any praise you have received. If anything, your customers will be annoyed. Don't go overboard. Show your pleasure but don't post about it again and again.

- Don't take it lightly – Since social media is aimed at building a community, initial activeness and then posting updates once in a blue moon is not good practice. Businesses using social media successfully are those that commit themselves to spending a certain amount of time organising their social media presence each day.

'Businesses using social media successfully are those that commit themselves to spending a certain amount of time organising their social media presence each day.'

With social media, there are boundless opportunities awaiting you to connect to prospects online. Following the simple dos and don'ts listed can ensure that your business reaps the best of social media marketing. Remember, it is only the right actions that can yield the right results.

Summing Up

- A business must choose the right form of social media to ensure success in conveying its message to its audience and meeting its customers' needs.

- Businesses must understand social media tools are not all equal, they all deliver different results subjective to the nature of the business.

- Combining the use of several different social media tools can be effective, but attempting to use them all can be extremely difficult and not produce the desired results.

- Launching a successful campaign via social media requires the business to know each one's particular specifications and to use these effectively and correctly.

- There are many dos and don'ts when it comes to using social media, which, if adhered to, will help your business reap the rewards.

Chapter Four

Social Media: Pros and Cons, and Winning Strategies

Pros and cons of different social media sites for business

When it comes to using social media for business, you can opt to avoid creating a Facebook page or an account on Twitter. However, you are giving your competitors a chance to stay ahead of you and reap benefits which you might otherwise claim. To top it all, you will be missing a great opportunity to market your business using exciting channels.

You will hear countless individuals singing praises for social media. Considering the amount of time people spend on these websites, it's hard not to get excited. Unfortunately, when it comes to social media, everyone does not agree it is a good idea to jump on the bandwagon.

Just as a coin has two sides, social media websites also have their share of highs and lows. It can be easily misused but when used correctly, social media can be a valuable addition to any marketing plan.

Do you want your business to have a social media presence just because every other business has one? As explained before, it cannot be denied that social media presence is an absolute must for any business to survive today. The question that needs to be answered is, which channels should be chosen?

'It can be easily misused but when used correctly, social media can be a valuable addition to any marketing plan.'

Websites like LinkedIn, Facebook and Twitter can be useful for several reasons, but they do have their negative attributes as well. Take time to investigate and determine which social media websites can help you fulfil your business goals.

The following briefly outlines the pros and cons of the most famous social media websites. There are a lot of factors that one has to take into consideration before signing up. This will help you evaluate if the good outweighs the bad or if it's the other way round.

Facebook – Social media king or an unrelenting sting?

According to recent statistics, users are believed to spend a total of 700 billion minutes on this website each month. The website's sharing feature has earned it great popularity. Nonetheless, any business looking to use Facebook for marketing should consider what it can share and how it can capitalise on it.

'Facebook offers a good opportunity for businesses to secure high visibility considering the number of people who use this website.'

Pros

- Facebook offers a good opportunity for businesses to secure high visibility considering the number of people who use this website.

- A Facebook user shares something on his wall. His friend decides to share it. Others who received it also decided to share it and this goes on and on. Imagine your popularity if that something shared virally is none other than your business's fan page.

Cons

- Your business posts can easily be lost among others posts on a News Feed. Remember you will be competing against photos or status updates by friends that are valued more.

- Negative comments are noticed at once. Make sure you have a 'terms of use' listed under your business's info. This will protect you in case you delete a comment.

Twitter – Tweet, bitter or sweet?

Cyberspace gets flooded with tweets in the event of any news-making development in our surroundings. This makes one wonder if Twitter can help any business grow one way or the other.

Surely, you cannot notify your followers of an upcoming earthquake. You can, however, give them something to value you for. Based on your offerings, you can produce content that strikes a chord with the readers and engages them.

Pros

- Interacting with your targeted market creates brand awareness for your business.

- Once you are able to engage prospects, you can then encourage them to respond to your call to action as desired.

Cons

- An endless stream of tweets means that yours can be easily ignored. Posting tweets at regular intervals will help you stay noticed.

- Since the character count is limited to 140, you need to have the ability to say a lot with a little. If 140 characters aren't sufficient, you can write an incomplete message that grabs attention. Just don't forget to include a link to the page or document where the complete story can be followed.

'An endless stream of tweets means that yours can be easily ignored. Posting tweets at regular intervals will help you stay noticed.'

LinkedIn – Link, as smart as you think?

LinkedIn is a networking website for professionals. Businesses can primarily use it to highlight their credentials.

Pros

- There is no fluff involved here. Your business's page will be clean, concise and professional. You can ask your employees to include background information about your company. You can also provide links to your blog's RSS, Facebook fan page or Twitter feed.

- It is easy to use. Once a business's page is set up, no other efforts are required.

Cons

- Traffic on LinkedIn is low. Also, engaging people so that they stay longer on your page is not as easy to accomplish as you may believe.

- LinkedIn is primarily used by professionals and business owners, so although it might be a great platform for B2B businesses, but it will only serve a niche market otherwise.

YouTube – Is a picture worth a thousand words?

With its massive influence, it is difficult to believe that YouTube is only seven years old. Statistics show that more than 3 billion videos are watched on YouTube each day. In addition, after Google, people prefer using YouTube to seek answers to their how-to queries or to meet any other information needs.

Pros

- You can communicate with consumers through videos. The idea is to create content that viewers find helpful. For instance, if you are selling household accessories, you can post videos on how to extend their life or the best way to keep them clean. You can also post videos promoting your products in an attractively humorous way.

- With attention span of individuals diminishing by the day, more and more businesses use visual aid to attract and retain a customer's interest level, and YouTube provides a great platform for that.

Cons

- It takes a lot of time and effort to edit or record a video. It may take even longer to come up with a unique idea for one. You have to ensure that any idea is worth the effort and time you invest into it.

- Making videos can be quite costly and will require a lot of planning and production hassles.

Organising social media outreach – A look at winning strategies

Social media allows a business to go beyond the walls and build relationships that are long lasting. Any efforts made in the direction should not be aimed at one-time communication. The real power of social media lies in its ability to allow businesses to know their contacts at a more personal level time and again. It is at this point that your ability to maintain and manage relationships comes into play as a company learns to cater to consumers' needs as they change over time.

Running blindly into the eye of the storm won't help. If you really want your marketing strategy to score, you not only need a strategic approach but a well-mapped plan in place as well. While there are several social networks you can choose from, Facebook, Twitter and LinkedIn are the most effective ones when it comes to connecting with people you don't know personally.

In the following section, you will learn how to leverage these networks to develop a beneficial business-customer relationship.

Building relationships on Twitter

All tweets aren't created equal. Businesses need to learn to share content in a way that it spikes their popularity. Imagine the scenario. You tweeted a link to an article. This will serve as your seal of approval for the author's work but this is where most businesses make mistakes. Your role doesn't end here. Tweeting a link isn't enough.

It will take you two seconds to tweet a link, it will take fifteen to pull out your favourite line from the content and it will take less than a minute to craft a genuine feedback. It comes as no surprise that the tweet with your take on the article will grab the most attention. The more time you invest in creating an attractive tweet, the more it will reflect your personality and the higher will be the response.

In order to get the hang of the microblogging business, consider the following tips that can help your tweet get responded:

'While there are several social networks you can choose from, Facebook, Twitter and LinkedIn are the most effective ones when it comes to connecting with people you don't know personally.'

- It is foolish to give publication credit instead of the author. Bear in mind that it is the author who structured the content, not the publication, and therefore, he/she should be the one getting all the appreciation.

- Have an opinion about everything you are tweeting. Appending it to anything you tweet will increase its appeal.

- Express what you liked or disliked about the information and support it with logical reasoning.

- Give creativity a chance. Instead of tweeting the article's title as it is, you can pique a reader's interest by quoting a particular line you found amusing in the article.

- People seek answers to queries and if you can them bait them using some useful tip provided in the article, there is no reason they won't respond to it.

- You can counter the point made in the article but tread carefully. Disagreement may jeopardise your relationship with the author.

- No one is interested in what someone said a year ago. Staying current and keeping your followers up to date is what works. Choose something that was written only a month back or so.

- Relevancy cannot be emphasised enough. If you deal in rental cars, who cares about the most amazing tips to keep their house clutter-free? Stay focused at your pitch.

'No one is interested in what someone said a year ago. Staying current and keeping your followers up to date is what works.'

The strategies listed above can help you build some buzz for your business. Give ingenuity a chance and build your web presence around simple and effective practices that others overlooked. Try to achieve the right balance of value and attraction in your tweets and you are all set to go.

Building relationships on LinkedIn

LinkedIn is the place where you will get a good idea of your prospective customers' (connections) professional ambitions and how your business will fit into the scenario. Most businesses believe the feat to accomplish is getting maximum connections. While it cannot be denied that connections do give your credibility and visibility a boost, the story doesn't end there. The principal challenge is to strengthen those connections to the point where people trust you enough to buy from you whatever it is you are selling.

Business success on LinkedIn goes hand in hand with relationships. With every single meaningful relationship you successfully create on this platform, you are a step closer to success. The million dollar question is what can you do to leverage these relationships? How can they significantly contribute to help you and your business excel? Keep reading to find out how LinkedIn can help you unlock countless opportunities.

Event leveraging

Stay abreast of your connections' whereabouts and keep a close eye on what they are doing. Since you are connected to them online, there is a fair chance you will easily get to know any events they are attending. If they are being hosted in your area or neighbourhood, you should attend them too. These events will be live and will serve as the perfect opportunity to interact with your connections face-to-face.

Take time to visit the RSVP page of the event as it will help you determine who among your connections will be present. You can then send those connections a message through InMail that you look forward to meeting them in person. This approach is quite effective.

Timing is all that matters

Time can play a paramount role when it comes to strengthening a relationship. Do it while you are still on your connection's mind. After you've made a new relation, introducing yourself and responding to a question or query, are all ideal scenarios to reach out and work towards a relationship that is meaningful. Such online interactions can result in discussions, phone calls and meetings.

'Business success on LinkedIn goes hand in hand with relationships. With every single meaningful relationship you successfully create on this platform, you are a step closer to success.'

Seek advice

Who doesn't want to give his/her two cents? After all, it makes you feel valued. You can score by reaching out to your connections and asking for their opinion about something. Not only will it make your connection feel valued, you will be amazed at the invaluable responses you will receive. Just make sure that when you reach out, you clearly explain who you are, inform the connection of any common thread between you both, pay a compliment and then tell the connection why you are seeking their point of view. This approach can easily help you spell success.

Be a meaningful resource

The idea is to make your connections perceive you as an SME (subject matter expert). Once you accomplish that, you will be the first name to pop in their minds in case they need advice or help. The more you are valuable to a connection, the more he/she will be motivated to work with you. Pay attention to their topic of discussion, status updates or any questions they post. The deeper you achieve an understanding of their issues, the more authoritative your advice will be for them. In order to build a meaningful relationship, your connections need to learn to trust you. Try to create opportunities to interact with your connections not just online but offline as well.

'LinkedIn is, beyond a doubt, one of the most powerful social media channels that exists today. It is critical to establish quality connections. The stronger the connection, the more successful your business will be.'

LinkedIn is, beyond a doubt, one of the most powerful social media channels that exists today. It is critical to establish quality connections but at the same time, the importance of strengthening these relationships cannot be underestimated. The stronger the connection, the more successful your business will be. There are valuable connections all around you. Just reach out and make the most of them.

Building relationships on Facebook

We all know that Facebook can be the perfect remedy to cure an ailing business. We also know how the social media giant can decide your business's fate. Keeping than in mind, the question is how to tackle this ever growing source of traffic so that it is the most profitable for your business.

From an online marketing standpoint, businesses that have set new records of success are those that have learned to unleash the Facebook magic. Whether it is about increasing your web traffic or securing better conversion rates, Facebook's outreach has earned it a reputation that is not going to wane anytime soon.

Creating long-term relationships with your prospects is what a business needs in order to succeed. By developing these relationships, it is possible to inspire loyalty and customer satisfaction, the core values needed by any business to float its boat.

Once you have a Facebook fan page in place, the next step is strengthening relationships to the extent that prospects know they can trust you for any of their needs.

The following will reveal some of the most useful strategies to build and cultivate customer relationships online.

Prioritise how you wish to engage

In order to engage fans, you first have to make up your mind about what you want to accomplish through your business's fan page. Do you:

- Want people to update posts on your page?
- Want people to genuinely compliment your services or products by leaving feedback?
- Want to spread the word about your offerings?
- Want people to purchase from your page?
- Want to create brand awareness by having mass exposure?

Whatever it is that you desire, once you are clear about your business goals, the rest is easy. Remember, each of the actions listed above needs you to take a different path and will earn a different value to your business.

'From an online marketing standpoint, businesses that have set new records of success are those that have learned to unleash the Facebook magic.'

Identifying important fans

It is no secret that not all fans are equal. Just as a company has a list of top customers, you also need to identify your top social media fans. These are people who are not only the most active but also perform all those activities that you have defined valuable. Once you have identified them, you can then formulate strategies to reach them.

Give value

Offering a loyalty programme is a commonly used tactic. You can cultivate one on Facebook too. Those that are playing a role to take you to the top deserve some sort of recognition. After you identify your top fans and the most important activities, you can please them further. For instance, if you want to create brand awareness, you can ask your fans to share your fan page with ten of their friends and they will get a, say, 20% discount on your offerings. This will delight your fans well beyond your expectations.

Communicate

It is vital that you communicate the value you are offering to each one of your fans. Clearly define terms of use and impose a limit on the number of times they can participate in an activity. This will also encourage any inactive fans to step ahead. Last but not the least, it is your responsibility to let your fans know about any new products, services, contents or sales you have launched.

In short, one can say that Facebook can help you develop long-term relationships with people you may have never met in person. You may only interact with them online but it will create a strong bond with the passage of time.

Just remember that relationships are not built overnight. It takes a lot of time and effort to nurture them into fulfilling and meaningful ones. When that happens, there will be no stopping you!

Finding your target audience on social media – An effort to excel

Finding and expanding your target audience is probably going to be one of the biggest challenges you will come across on your road to growing your business through social media. Nonetheless, what cannot be questioned is social media's competency in achieving business goals.

A mistake common to most business owners is that they fail to understand the difference between traffic and relevant traffic. The idea is not to reach as many people as you can but reaching individuals that are interested in your offerings and can help you grow. This is where the challenge lies.

As a savvy marketer, the responsibility falls on your shoulder to find out who and where these people are. To help you accomplish just that, there are different applications and platforms that can be used to identify and create a win-win situation for both the parties. Using these tools, you will be at an advantage as here is where you will be the one holding all the aces. The list goes as follows.

HootSuite – Hit right on target

HootSuite is one of the most practical social media management tools available to date. It allows you to streamline multi-user collaboration and facilitates the management of multiple social media accounts, giving the manager utmost control over all the happenings surrounding his business; but apart from being a great platform to manage, it is also remarkable when it comes to monitoring the social media space.

You can set up what is known as 'streams' which is essentially defining your channels for updates on the basis of the preferences you set. For instance, if you want to view Twitter for mentions of a specific keyword or phrase associated to your business, you can do so with HootSuite.

Using this stream, you can unveil several opportunities to determine and engage your target audience. There are several filters such as sentiment or location that can help you derive more relevant results.

'A mistake common to most business owners is that they fail to understand the difference between traffic and relevant traffic.'

Twilert – A signal for success

This tool gives you the ability to monitor Twitter for a specific hashtag, phrase or @mention. You will receive emails notifying you of any relevant findings at regular intervals. What this means is you can view Twitter continuously and react to any mentions of a specific keyword or phrase quickly.

In addition, what further makes Twitter possibly the best prospecting tool ever is that the information is open for all to see! Unlike other platforms where permission is needed to follow someone, there are no such restrictions with Twitter.

Businesses can take advantage of this situation to find the individuals who are following their competitors. If people are following them, there is a big chance people might be interested in following you too.

What you can do is to create a private list and add these people to this list. You can then keep an eye on how your competitors are interacting with these individuals to seek opportunities to engage.

Facebook Ads – Target to market

Facebook has produced tremendous results for some brands, while others are still trying to get things going for them. The most appealing feature Facebook has incorporated is ads that are highly targeted.

Every attribute you can possibly think of can be used to display advertisements to specific audiences. This criterion includes age, marital status, education, location, employer, friends of those who liked your page, upcoming birthdays, etc.

Using the right combination of filters, you can easily gain exposure to only those who will be interested. At the very least, you will be able to drive groups of people to your website or fan page.

LinkedIn – Planning for possibilities

If you want relevant traffic rather than good-for-nothing visitors, LinkedIn can be a choice that can never go wrong. With a premium account on this platform, you can generate leads using a variety of filters such as interests, company size, experience, seniority, your groups and others.

Even if you do not have a premium account, you can still initiate searches for contacts or specific companies. You cannot only connect to these individuals, you can also seek their introduction from the network.

To top it all, you can use LinkedIn to find any people who have any queries regarding your market niche. By assisting them, you not only gain trust but also establish the desired bond easily.

Remember, regardless of the social media channels you choose to market your business, there is one thing that you have to provide, that's value. You can provide it in the form of a solution to a problem or content. This is because without providing value you do not stand a chance of engaging your prospects and, if you fail to engage prospects, there's no way you will be able to generate business.

'If you want relevant traffic rather than good-for-nothing visitors, LinkedIn can be a choice that can never go wrong.'

Summing Up

- If you choose not to use social networking sites such as Facebook and Twitter, you are immediately giving your competitors the edge over your business.

- Each form of social media has its associated pros and cons. It's important you research them thoroughly so you can choose the most suitable for your particular business.

- Facebook, Twitter and LinkedIn are considered to be the best social networks for connecting with people you don't know personally.

- Learning to use these correctly and building effective relationships on each of them will ensure you'll generate successful business and promote beneficial business-customer relationships.

Chapter Five

Facebook User Manual

Despite the massive popularity of the social media network, organisations and businesses are unsure as to how to unleash the 'Facebook effect'. For the convenience of business owners, we have established a comprehensive guide where readers will learn how to set up their page, use it to gain exposure and connect to their customers.

This guide will start with the basics, such as the creation of an attractive fan page to draw in the right prospects. Moving ahead, the guide will reveal how businesses can use sponsored stories and ads to boost their online image. Finally, we will take a look at some strategies to evolve a Facebook page into a richer platform with marketing at the heart of it.

Facebook – The key to an excelling enterprise

Customers are the heart and soul of any business and it is these customers that make or break any business. That's why, it is inevitable to build relationships with your prospects, reach new but relevant people and drive the desired sales.

'According to statistics, 3.2 billion likes and comments are made by users each day on Facebook.'

According to statistics, 3.2 billion likes and comments are made by users each day on Facebook. This should help you realise the sheer power of having an impressive presence on Facebook. When your business is the topic of conversation, you have every reason to celebrate as your business is using the full potential of word-of-mouth marketing or to put it simply, recommendation.

When it comes to securing success for a business on Facebook, the entire process can be divided into three simple and effective steps briefly outlined on the following pages. Following these steps, any business owner can fulfil any dreams he/she has had about their business. Using these steps, any business, irrespective of its scope or nature, can easily become the talk of the town.

Step 1 – Build your page

Just as Facebook users have a profile to represent them, businesses need to create a fan page as this is where they will make efforts to build brand, foster relationships or simply grow business.

Creating a Facebook page

'Just as Facebook users have a profile to represent them, businesses need to create a fan page as this is where they will make efforts to build brand, foster relationships or simply grow business.'

Facebook pages can be created free of charge and all it takes is a few minutes to get started. In order to create a page, navigate to the URL: www.facebook.com/pages/create.php. Once on this page, the next step is choosing a certain category for your page such as local business, brand/product and others. The steps that follow are listed below:

- Choose a page name and category to represent your business.
- Pick an image or logo representing your business. It will be used as your profile picture.
- Write a brief description to tell people what your business is all about.
- Think of a web address for your fan page that you can use on multiple platforms to inform customers of your Facebook presence.
- Choose a cover photo you find fitting to represent your services or products. Remember it is going to be the first things users will notice upon arrival on your page.

You can edit content on your page, respond to messages, view insights and keep an eye on activity through the Admin Panel.

You will find the Edit Page option in the Admin Panel. Using it you can update information or any other details about your business.

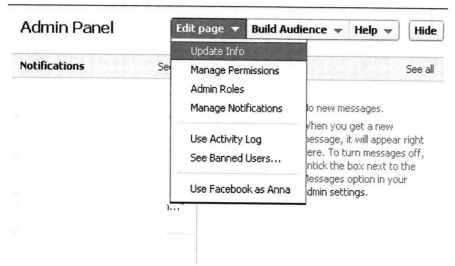

Creating your first Facebook post

You are now all set to create the first post for your page. It is important to understand at this point that there are different kinds of posts such as photos, questions, videos and updates. Those who have liked your page will now see your posts in News Feed.

Understanding the News Feed

News Feed is actually the centre of the entire Facebook experience. This is where your prospects will be able to see any posts you have made on your page.

News feed is of utmost importance as this is where people spend around 40% of their time on Facebook. Also, this is where users share their real-life experiences and opinions and this is where you can engage them.

'News Feed is actually the centre of the entire Facebook experience. This is where your prospects will be able to see any posts you have made on your page.'

Creating successful posts

While Facebook has earned some brands success overnight, there are those still trying to get to grips with it. This happens because they are unaware of the three qualities of a post that can tempt any user into reading and responding to it. These are:

- Short – Posts that are clear and concise never fail to strike a chord with anyone. Statistics show that posts having a word count of 100-250 characters are the ones to get 60% more shares, comments and likes.

- Visual – Who can resist a visual treat? If user engagement is your goal, pictures, videos and albums get 120%, 100% and 180% more of it respectively.

- Optimised – You will come across Page Insights where you can find information such as the peak time people responded to the content you published. Using this information, you can remember posting during those specific hours.

How to make people 'like' your page

Once you have set up a page and started posting, the next milestone to accomplish is getting the maximum 'likes' for your page. You are most likely to have a community of family, friends, employees or customers who are interested in your business. Your job is to persuade them to 'like' your page. There are several things you can try to achieve that.

- You can make use of the Build Audience button you will find at the Admin Panel. First and foremost, make sure you invite your Facebook friends to 'like' your page. You can move ahead from there onwards.

- You can opt for the 'Invite Email Contacts' option. This will upload your email list and you will be able to send a message requesting people to like your page.

- You can use your fan page's address on receipts, chalkboards, store signs, emails, business cards or any other marketing material you have in place.

Step 2 – Connecting with people

With a Facebook fan page in place, it is now time to direct all your efforts towards reaching new and existing potential prospects. The idea is to attract people you believe are the perfect fit for your business. This is done through Facebook Ads. In this section, we will shed some light on how you can create ads on Facebook.

Creating ads on Facebook

Ads on Facebook are messages from businesses that are paid. You can also incorporate the social context into it because statistics show that people who are connected to you on Facebook are twice as likely to convert into customers as compared to those who don't know you. Read on to go through a step-by-step guide of reaching the right people through ads.

Setting up your first ad

First and foremost, you have to select a page you wish to promote.

Next, you will come across several options under 'what would you like to do?' Things you can do include:

* Get more page likes – This option should be chosen if you want to connect to people who haven't liked your page already. Once you choose this option, you will be requested to start designing your ad. This will include three basic tasks: thinking of an attractive headline, creating body text and choosing a catchy image.

* Promote page posts – If your principal goal is promoting a particular post, this option will help you achieve so. Using it, you not only ensure improved reach but significantly increase your chances of finding prominent position in the News Feed as well.

* Advanced options – You will also come across this option where you will be able to see all bidding and creative options. You have the flexibility to choose Cost per Click (CPC) or Cost per Mile (CPM).

'Statistics show that people who are connected to you on Facebook are twice as likely to convert into customers as compared to those who don't know you.'

Reaching the right audience

A business can only flourish by reaching potential prospects. While creating brand awareness does work in your favour, it is ultimately the sales secured by a company that can take it to the next level. When it comes to reaching the right people for your business, the following tips can prove to be invaluable:

- You should have a good idea of who can be your ideal customer. This is because, once you have selected your sponsored stories and ads, you will have to decide who you want to see it.

- Another factor that comes into play is the audience size. It is the number that specifies how many people will see your ad if you have sufficient budget and bid.

- There are countless attributes you can use to target your demographics such as gender, age and location.

Initiating your Facebook campaign – Scheduling and pricing

- Start with naming your campaign. You then have to decide how much you want to invest into the campaign as well as the time when you want to launch it.

- By default, you will be using the Cost per Mile (CPM) payment option unless you have opted for Advanced Options in the section under 'goals'.

- Your ad will automatically be optimised according to the details you have specified so that you reach people who can help your business grow.

- Probably, what attracts most business owners is that they never have to go beyond their means in their effort to market. The amount a business owner agrees to pay will be fixed as per his/her specifications to reach only those to whom your offerings matter.

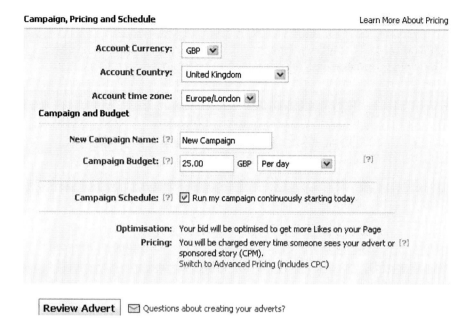

Campaign, Pricing and Schedule   Learn More About Pricing

Account Currency:	GBP ▼
Account Country:	United Kingdom ▼
Account time zone:	Europe/London ▼

Campaign and Budget

| New Campaign Name: [?] | New Campaign |
| Campaign Budget: [?] | 25.00 | GBP | Per day ▼ | [?] |

| Campaign Schedule: [?] | ☑ Run my campaign continuously starting today |

Optimisation: Your bid will be optimised to get more Likes on your Page

Pricing: You will be charged every time someone sees your advert or [?] sponsored story (CPM).
Switch to Advanced Pricing (includes CPC)

Review Advert | ✉ Questions about creating your adverts?

Testing multiple ads

If you think all ads are the same, you are in for a big surprise. Audiences respond to different ads differently, and running different versions of the same ad can be a smart approach as you can determine what the audience is most responsive to. In the following example, we have used different graphics for the two ads targeting the same audience to find out which one will steal the show. While doing so, you should take the following factors into consideration:

* Rest and take time to control – Make sure you have the original version of the ad so as to control and test any changes you have made.

* Modify only one part of the ad – Since you are trying to determine the aspects impacting the response most, it is recommended that you only change one part of your ad at a time as it will help you understand what actually drives audience.

* Creating several versions of the same ad – You can replicate your ad by

choosing 'Create a Similar Ad' for a particular ad in Ads Manager. Ads Manager is a simple plug-in which provides space for online advertisements. It is a very helpful tool and can be very useful in operating multiple advertisements and tracking their performances on Facebook.

Facebook is a smart choice for businesses because when you have several ads running in a marketing campaign, your daily budget is automatically allocated to ads that are performing best. That's why it is important that your ads are placed in multiple campaigns when you are testing them for performance.

'Facebook is a smart choice for businesses because when you have several ads running in a marketing campaign, your daily budget is automatically allocated to ads that are performing best.'

Measurable performance

Now that you have designed your ads, the next step is monitoring their performance using Ads Manager. This will give you a fair idea of what will work best for your audience so that the stipulated budget is spent in the best possible manner.

Step 3 – Engaging your audience

When you generate posts consistently, it leads to conversions. You build loyalty and countless opportunities to create sales. In this section, we will elaborate on what you can do to achieve superior user engagement.

Posting content regularly

When it comes to content, quality cannot be emphasised enough. When people like your page, they are giving the signal that your business matters to them and want to stay informed about what's going on. Quality and relevance are the two most important factors in this regard.

Writing quality posts

If you want to know what you can do to write posts that will make a difference, keep the following tips in mind:

- Posts should always be relevant to your business and audience.

- Try to be as conversational and friendly as possible.

- Share videos and photos as they are known to secure higher user engagement.

- You can seek input from your audience or ask question.

- In order to offer value to customers, share exclusive information about any deals or discounts.

- For an online business, keeping customers up to date will make them trust you even more. Share news, current events or holidays.

Attract your audience with offers

You have to continuously think of ways to pique your audience's interest. What you can do is to reach them with a certain offer exclusively for those who have liked your page. You can also ask them to share it on their timeline or with other friends who might be interested.

It is strongly suggested that you post at least once or twice each week to stay relevant and in the mind of those who want to know more about you.

Promoting posts to reach people

Promoting your post is one of the easiest ways to reach your targeted demographics. By choosing to promote your post, you can make it more prominent than it would have been on News Feed.

This means that you will actually be increasing chances of people viewing your post in their News Feed. They will be informed of your web presence and will be more likely to respond to whatever sales promotion or offer it is.

Understanding how to improve your reach in the News Feed

Let's say for instance there is a user named Anna. She had her friend's wedding this week and all the other friends are posting excitedly about it. In this scenario, because of the higher engagement of friends, their posts will be shown on top of her News Feed.

This means that your business page may not get the exposure it previously used to. It won't appear that often or it will appear but it will be below those friends' stories. This is where the option to promote your post comes into play. By using it, you will appear higher on Anna's News Feed than is possible otherwise.

Understanding Page Insights

Page Insights helps you evaluate the posts that are working most effectively for those connected to you. Savvy marketers recommend that you check these insights on a regular basis to find out if things are responding in the desired manner. If you think this option will only be available to those with thousands of likes, in actual fact those with as few as 30 likes can use it. In case you do not even have 30 likes, you can always use the option 'Invite People to Like Your Page'.

Responding to your audience

One of the most fruitful practices on Facebook is to stay in a constant dialogue with your audience. Responding here defines three tasks:

- Making efforts to engage – If you want to encourage people to start a relationship with your page, you have to constantly strive to engage. This means that you respond to any private messages or queries at once.

- Address particular people – You can address people specifically by tagging them using @ before their name in case several people have commented on your post. People will appreciate it that you are taking time to specifically answer them.

- Keep track of all your messages – When people send private messages, a notification pops up in the Admin Panel. This helps you to keep track of those who are interested in your offerings and by responding to them, you can let audience know that you are listening.

'One of the most fruitful practices on Facebook is to stay in a constant dialogue with your audience.'

Summing Up

- Marketing on Facebook can help any business grow if done correctly and effectively.

- The key to creating a successful Facebook marketing campaign consists of three simple steps:

    1. Construct a page that looks professional and helps build your brand, customer relationships and your business.

    2. Connect with people by placing effective ads on Facebook Ads.

    3. Engage with your audience through consistent, appealing, quality posts and use your customers' News Feeds to their full potential.

- Creating a successful Facebook campaign for your business will help establish you as a professional and allow you to be in constant communication with your audience/consumers, building valuable trust between you.

Chapter Six

LinkedIn User Manual

LinkedIn is the exceptional social networking site that can help businesses secure rare benefits. Building a specialised collaborative network for professionals and executives, LinkedIn helps businesses grow by developing the right connections and partnerships. The corporate networking site has allowed many businesses to get off the ground by leveraging its potential.

This chapter is aimed to help you realise how easily LinkedIn can be used and addresses other finer points as well that the majority of business owners fail to understand. By the end of this section, the incredible potential of this site will be revealed to you and you will be eager to use it for your business.

We'll start off with the basics and define different terminologies in the context of this particular networking site.

'LinkedIn helps businesses grow by developing the right connections and partnerships.

Network: Every individual is the centre of his network and there are multiple concentric circles around him.

Connection: Connections in this manual will be used to refer to first level relationship with those in your network.

Introductions: They are essentially requests that are used to communicate to any members you aren't directly connected to. It is important to bear in mind that members can only have limited introductions pending at a time.

InMail: They are messages that sponsored LinkedIn members are allowed to send to anyone on the network. The level of membership you opt for has a specific number of InMails that can be sent each month. A perk is that the sender need not necessarily have information about the recipient as LinkedIn serves as the intermediary. If you receive an InMail, you are allowed to take three actions. You can reject it, you can choose to reject any InMails from that person in future or you can initiate a conversation with the sender. Finally, you can completely opt out of receiving any InMails altogether.

Forwarder: This is the term used for a connection that chose to forward your request to one of his/her contacts.

Other Contacts: Little is known about this terminology. Actually when you the import contacts on LinkedIn, all your contacts will be listed as Other Contacts. From there, you can choose contacts you wish become your first connections. You can invite these people individually and even if they do not respond to your invitation, you will be notified whenever they join the network.

'First degree connections are the strongest ties you have on LinkedIn.'

Understanding different network levels

It is important to understand that when it comes to LinkedIn, there are four views worth mentioning arranged in their order of visibility.

- Your network (it includes the first, second and third degree connections. See the next section for more on these.)

- LinkedIn network

- The non-LinkedIn network

- The non-networked network

Your network

This is where you can directly communicate with your first degree connections. As far as the second and third degree connections go, you can only view certain information for those who fall in that area. For instance:

- First degree connections are the strongest ties you have on LinkedIn.

- When you want to connect to someone who's connected to any of your connections, you request an introduction from your connection. This first degree connection helps you communicate with your desired new connection. Look at it this way. Betty is the second degree person I wish to reach and I am connected to her through Barbara. You write a note to Betty stating as to why you wish to connect to her. You also write a note to Barbara requesting an introduction. Now Barbara reads both those notes and can choose to forward them to Betty or not. The procedure is same when you wish to reach a third degree connection.

- It is important to remember that many can see the requests you make and the way you communicate with others. Also, if you help others achieve their business goals, they will reciprocate in the same manner.

The LinkedIn network

Your LinkedIn network resides outside your third degree connections. However, you can only communicate with them provided you have upgraded your membership. For instance, as a member holding the business membership, the searches you will initiate will not only return results for those in your network but for those in your LinkedIn network as well, according to the specified criteria. Personal members (free subscribers), on the other hand, can only see results relevant to their network.

Now consider this scenario, you sell car tyres. A French car seller is not a part of your network and that's why only the company name, info and type will be visible to you. As a business member, you can send three InMails. This means each month you can reach three connections you do not know. You can send the French car seller an InMail. If he/she wishes to communicate, you can then both become first degree connections. This way the process goes on.

Non-LinkedIn networks

You can take a step ahead by inviting people who have not yet subscribed to LinkedIn. The network effect comes into play here because a network's value increases with an increase in the number of people who are a part of it. Since we know that leaders of the older generation are more sceptical about the use of digital social networks, it is vital that they are represented on this network.

Membership fees and types

As an effort to help you get an insight into the various deals that are available to you, below is the membership comparison chart. While you can build a robust network of personal connections free of charge, paid memberships have countless perks. This is particularly useful in the case when you don't have several trusted contacts to expand your network. The different memberships offered are listed as follows:

'While you can build a robust network of personal connections free of charge, paid memberships have countless perks.'

Compare Plans	Basic	Business	Business Plus	Executive
Pricing: Annual | Monthly		US$24.95/MO	US$49.95/MO	US$99.95/MO
		Start Now	Start Now	Start Now
Visibility				
Who's Viewed My Profile Get the complete list of who's viewed your profile, how they found you, their industries etc.	Limited	✓	✓	✓
Full Profiles Access to full profiles of anyone in your entire network.	Limited up to 2nd degree	✓	✓	✓
Full Name Visibility See names of your 3rd-degree and group connections				✓
Search				
Premium Search Get advanced search filters, more results, and search results		✓	✓	✓
Profiles Per Search Up to 7x more profiles when you search	100	300	500	700
Search Alerts Automatic alerts when profiles meet your saved search criteria	3 weekly	5 weekly	7 weekly	10 weekly
Reference Search Get a list of people to refer someone you're interested in		✓	✓	✓
Reach				
InMail Messages Send direct messages to anyone on LinkedIn Response guaranteed		3 per month	10 per month	25 per month
Company Introductions Get introduced to inside sources at companies through someone you already know on LinkedIn	5	10	15	25
OpenLink Let anyone message you for free when you activate OpenLink.		✓	✓	✓
Management				
Profile Organizer Save profiles, create folders to manage your pipeline		5 folders	25 folders	50 folders
Priority Customer Service		✓	✓	✓

Membership comparison

If you are wondering about the membership you should sign up for, there are certain differences you need to notice: the number of InMails, introductions and network results. If you opt for free membership, you can still effectively build a productive network while making use of the majority of LinkedIn tools. However, problems will arise when you try to reach someone outside your LinkedIn network. You won't be allowed to send/receive InMails and plenty of contacts you can use for your business won't show up in search results.

Creating your networking

In the world we live in, business relationships need to succeed and you can take the first step in that direction by joining LinkedIn. You can do so in one of the following suggested manners.

Log on to www.LinkedIn.com. You can then create your company's profile in three simple steps:

- Go to the 'Companies' menu on LinkedIn. Next, you have to click on 'Add Company'.

- You will be asked to provide basic information such as your company's description, the industry you are operating in, the number of employees you have and so on.

- Last but not the least, we recommend you to take assitane from LinkedIn's wizards for the creation of company profile because not only will you be able to add locations, feed and logo for your company's profile, you can avail countless other opportunities as well.

Once your company's LinkedIn profile is created, you can move ahead and start sending out invitations or you can respond to an invitation you have received to join LinkedIn and can then carry out the task of profile creation and sending invitations.

If you opt for the first route, a profile will be created but there won't be any connections. Opting for the second one, you will already have a connection – the one who has invited you.

To invite others to join the network, reach them through email by clicking on 'Know this person? Add them as a 'Connection' link.

The foundation of LinkedIn network – Building a community

The importance of choosing the right connections cannot be emphasised enough. Community building revolves around two principal strategies: higher number of connections with loose ties and lower number of connections with strong ties. Since not everything works for everyone, we have briefly identified the advantages of each.

'The importance of choosing the right connections cannot be emphasised enough.'

- Your network is essentially a community you are building. This means that before starting off with the task, you should have a vision and a purpose to do it.

For instance, imagine you have invited several people to join the network. You have known them for years and have interests similar to them. This could be a great start towards a strong-ties strategy. You may have a limited reach in the beginning but you are at an advantage here as well. Your connections won't be hesitant to forward introductions. They will ultimately prove to the stimulus you require to facilitate your goal of finding an employee, investor or job opportunity.

- An important aspect is making someone who has requested an introduction your priority. If you show others that you are taking things seriously, others will be encouraged to help you pave your path towards success as well. Don't forget, the way you communicate with your network will determine your community's culture. As you sow, so shall you reap.

- Don't forget to spend a certain amount of time and go though LinkedIn Answers. Try to find out how you can make the most out of this feature. If you want your connections to provide valuable insight into your matters and serve as a personal advisory board, it can turn out to be a guiding principle that a strategy to form strong ties will work best for you.

- If your goals are not yet clear and the relationships you want to form are those with young and energetic professionals, a strategy to form loose ties will work better. This is because you get a chance to expand your network more.

▨ Try to imagine where you would like to see your community/network standing a year or two from now. What are your business goals? Who are the people you wish to see in your network? What do you want your nature of interaction to be? What will be appreciated by those you are trying to reach?

Maximising return on investment (ROI)

It is no secret that higher ROI is the ultimate goal of every business making use of any of the social media platforms. By encouraging trustworthy relations between consumers and businesses, social media strives to develop an environment where all consumers' needs are met with satisfaction.

When it comes to LinkedIn, it is trust that holds everything together in place. It is a rule of thumb to not have plenty of connections if you are not comfortable with the idea of referring or recommending them to someone else. Your first degree connections should always be those you can have reciprocal relationships with as these are the people who can actively help you attain your goals. Members can connect to other members only by following specific rules.

'When it comes to LinkedIn, it is trust that holds everything together in place.'

There are a variety of ways a business can use LinkedIn. The following briefly describes the four business models that every business can use. If you are still hesitant about using it, the following will help you understand why investing in LinkedIn is a smart business move. The models are arranged in the level of activity, lowest to the highest. Some models are also used in conjunction with other ones.

Professional presence

Regardless of your profession or business, there will always be people you are no longer in touch with. By creating a profile on LinkedIn, you not only allow people to get in touch with you but you can further grow your network using introductions and InMails. If someone contacts you and you do not appreciate their effort to connect, you can block them entirely from contacting you in the future.

- ▪ Focus – Allows people to find you.

- ▪ Time investment – Spend 1-3 hours each week on LinkedIn for this model to be employed in the desired manner. Also, spending a certain amount of time each month engaging in the recommended activities will also boost your LinkedIn presence.

- ▪ ROI – A LinkedIn profile is not something created just because everyone else is doing so. It is one of the most effective means of meteorically increasing your business's reach and uncovering an assortment of opportunities.

- ▪ Critical factors for success – When it comes to identifying factors that can help you secure success, quality profile is on top of the list. This is because outlining your talents and professional interests will allow you to discover more opportunities.

Network management

The second model that needs to be discussed here is network management. Unlike the model discussed previously, in network management the emphasis is on building connections with those who already know you on this platform. LinkedIn helps you to stay connected to everyone regardless of how geographically apart people are from you.

- ▪ Focus – Self-management of a network that can be expanded.

- ▪ Time investment – Spending 1-3 hours weekly can work wonders. It is also strongly suggested that in order to manage the network competently, spending at least 2 hours sending out invitations and writing recommendations can help you improve business reach immensely.

- ▪ ROI – By using this model, you will be able to interact with others at a more personal level. You will be able to easily monitor all the activities in your

'By creating a profile on LinkedIn, you not only allow people to get in touch with you but you can further grow your network using introductions and InMails.'

contacts' circle. All you have to do is to enable notifications when any of your connections perform some sort of activity and several opportunities will start surfacing on their own.

- Critical factors for success – Factors that define success for this particular model include an excellently maintained profile and usage of a clear message offering value when inviting people.

Network building

When it comes to network building, all efforts are directed towards increasing the number of contacts you have. LinkedIn has uses in a large variety of areas. If you are an entrepreneur, you can use LinkedIn's potential to create connections to help you form ventures or secure deals. A fool-proof tip is to use particular words and phrases when creating your profile as it helps people reach and search for you easily.

- Focus – This model solely serves the purpose of building network proactively. While doing so, businesses can drive new opportunities in different areas associated to their field of work. To accomplish this, you can write recommendations or express your opinion at LinkedIn Answers.

- Time investment – This model requires you to spend at least 4 to 6 hours each week performing tasks like sending out invitations and engaging in conversations through LinkedIn Answers and writing recommendations.

- ROI – If you think you are spending a lot of time building your network, you have no idea how easily you are paving a path for your business to get off the ground. The best aspect about this model is opportunities increase with the expansion of network.

- Critical factors for success – The approach you are using to invite others should be compelling and convincing. Similarly, leadership qualities and mentoring network building closely are things to certainly work in your favour.

Network living

Network living is the model with the highest level of involvement. Here several other factors come into play as network building and management are the prime professional activities. In this regard, LinkedIn often becomes utterly indispensable for you and to you. Essentially, network building is a lot like network living except that the involvement is that of a higher degree.

- Focus – The way you maintain your LinkedIn network can directly influence the revenues generated. This suggests that you should be consistently making efforts to reach new people that can help your business grow. You can form collaborations with LinkedIn Corp to pilot any novel offerings that are being developed.

- Time investment – Since the results are more lucrative, the effort is that of a higher degree as well. It is recommended that you spend around 20 hours each week on the platform and have more than one LinkedIn profile. Make sure you do not forget to have one corporate profile.

- ROI – By now, you must have a clear idea of the amount of time you will need to spend on LinkedIn in order to monetise your interactions. Results on LinkedIn are measurable and it is in this manner that LinkedIn becomes a crucial part of this business.

- Critical factors for success – With this model, you have to let go of all conventionalism. Leadership, innovations and appropriate process execution are factors to help you succeed. You can start off by creating and measuring processes you have outlined previously. You are now responsible for executing them consistently. You can seek help from other connections as well, as these are the people who can understand in depth the variety of aspects of your LinkedIn activity.

Using the information in this chapter, we hope that you have now understood all that be done to make the most out of LinkedIn for businesses. Just decide what will work for you and you will soon be able to meet and exceed all expectations you have for your business.

Summing Up

⬚ LinkedIn is a corporate networking site for professionals and executives. It helps businesses grow by developing the right connections and building successful relationships.

⬚ Membership to LinkedIn is free, however free membership does have its restraints; paid membership affords countless perks.

⬚ Building your network on LinkedIn is essentially like building a community; you may have limited reach initially, but establishing strong relationships with the right connections and effective communication will lead to your network growing.

Chapter Seven

Twitter User Manual

You may not know but there are countless businesses out there who believe that a single tweet is all it takes for a small business to evolve into one that needs no introduction.

In present day and age, a single tweet can be the little thing that can make a big difference. Spurring all the online coverage any business can ask for, Twitter has not only galvanised unlimited success stories but has also given business owners a reason to consider it the strongest weapon they can have in their arsenal against competition.

Twitter is one of the most prominent, not to forget powerful, social media platforms today. With thousands of tweets flowing through it on every possible subject from every single corner of the world every minute, it's fair to say that businesses can use it to make their presence known.

Like many others, you must be aware of the fact that the biggest corporate giants are using it. It actually comes as a surprise that something with a tag line as simple as 'what are you doing?' can lead to such phenomenal results.

Like every other platform, Twitter also has its share of those who are skeptical about its efficacy. To those people, all we can say is there's more to Twitter than meets the eye. In fact, this is what this chapter is about. We will not only help you understand how you can use it better but also how your company/business can use it to enrich its client base. Basically, what you can actually accomplish through Twitter is amplifying your message and growing your business ultimately.

For your convenience, we have divided this guide into three main sections.

- Getting started – Many of your targeted audience are already using Twitter.

> 'Twitter is one of the most prominent, not to forget powerful, social media platforms today.'

This gives you the opportunity to engage them into a conversation. This section will help you fully comprehend how Twitter can be used to match business goals effectively.

▦ Engage your audience – Do you have any idea that it is the way you communicate that shapes your business's identity? Why not tweet about your business principles, ideas and the value your business has to offer. How about being an eye candy for prospects by sharing with them beneficial links and attractive pictures? Give your customers an insight into all that happens behind the scenes.

▦ Amplifying impact – It is obvious that the more people talk about your business on Twitter, the more customers or 'followers' you'll get. This section will explain the variety of activities that can be performed that will help you promote your username and expand your business. So, let's get started.

'Given the social media site's phenomenal popularity, it is of vital importance to learn what Twitter can do for your business and how you can effectively join a conversation.'

Getting started

Given the social media site's phenomenal popularity, it is of vital importance to learn what Twitter can do for your business and how you can effectively join a conversation. First and foremost, we look at the anatomy of a tweet. For someone new to Twitter, it will come in handy to know that tweets are the building blocks of communications on this platform. A tweet is indeed one of the best examples of saying more with less and the amazing responses you can generate through 140 characters or less are mind-boggling.

We'll now explain the illustration of the tweet on the previous page:

1. Hashtag

Any word that begins with the # sign is a hashtag. They are used for conversations that are directed at a particular topic. By clicking on the hashtag, you can view results for the specific term.

2. Mention

There are instances when you wish to bring your tweet to someone's attention. In this case, one should use mention instead of reply so that others are able to see it. Mention is used by using @ with the username of whoever it is you wish to converse with. Such tweets are displayed in the mentions section. All followers can see it and clicking on mention will take you to the individual's profile.

3. Reply

If you want to respond to someone in particular, make sure you use the 'reply' button. Replies are public by default and they will show up in your timeline as well as the recipient's timeline. Your response will also appear on the timeline of those following you or the recipient. This means that if someone is not in the conversation, he/she should follow both the individuals to keep track of their conversation.

4. Retweet

If some tweet can be of value to someone else, you can simply retweet it. Just hit the button and all of your followers will be able to see the original message.

5. Links

Since the restriction on the tweet is 140 characters and links are almost always longer than that, Twitter has incorporated a link-shortening feature so that a link of any size can be accommodated within the limit. Hootsuite also has this facility. If you would prefer to manually shorten the link, it can be copied and pasted into Tiny URL (www.tinyurl.com) which will then generate a shortened link.

Creating your account

- Log on to www.twitter.com. Click on the 'sign up' button provided at the home page. You will be asked to choose a username. While this username can be altered later on, it is recommended to get it right the first time as there is a chance search engines will be confused.

- Next step is confirming your account using CAPTHCHA. A CAPTHCHA is a 'challenge response' test used to ensure that the response is generated by a human being. For example, you may be asked to retype a set of characters and numbers (which have been randomly generated) displayed on the screen. This is actually done to ensure that the request is generated by a human and not a spam account made by programmed computers to accomplish so.

- The last step is adding the requested profile details.

'Your profile represents your business and you should be willing to go to any lengths to make it as aesthetically appealing as possible.'

Designing your profile

Your profile represents your business and you should be willing to go to any lengths to make it as aesthetically appealing as possible. Since your profile will help others' perceptions about your business, your name, website, profile picture and bio should all be elements telling your story effectively.

Choose a profile image that is strongly associated with your business

Include a link to your website

Write a clear and informative bio that describes your business, products or services

A background image offers a large opportunity for branding and helps set the tone for your profile page

Upload a profile header image that showcases your personality to immediately engage with your profile visitors

'Your account on Twitter is all about showing your business's personality. You need to have a certain style and voice for your business.'

Spice up your account

Your account on Twitter is all about showing your business's personality. You need to have a certain style and voice for your business. Since it is something that cannot be achieved overnight, it is understandable that it will take some time but you will be able to find your voice with constant use.

One other thing that you have to keep in mind is that any employees you have will most likely be using their personal accounts for tweeting. You can retweet them and explain in a friendly manner what they are talking about and how their tweets align with your business goals and interests.

When you are tweeting on behalf of your company or business, it is a must to use a friendly and conversational tone as it is appreciated.

Engaging your audience

Believe it or not, the right content can empower you to convert prospects into customers and customers into dedicated clientele. Now let's take a look at different audience-engaging activities.

Listen first

When you first start using Twitter, it can be difficult to stop yourself from tweeting right away. However, before you plunge into it, it is only smart to follow and closely observe what other similar businesses are doing. This effort can help you judge if something can work in your favour and you will be able to learn from their mistakes as well.

Following someone means you want to subscribe to anything they will be sharing via tweets. These tweets will automatically appear on your timeline. Similarly, if someone follows you, your tweets will appear on their timeline.

Perhaps the biggest advantage associated with Twitter is the asymmetrical model it uses for its followers. You don't need permissions or approvals and this transparent flow of information makes it a true blessing for businesses.

Twitter has been designed so that you are most likely to follow those following you. You not only acknowledge your followers in this manner but can also send/receive messages directly.

A good place to start is to search Twitter for all the terms relevant to your business. You can then use the results to determine what people are saying about similar businesses and the strategies they are using for better user engagement. You can also learn a lot from comments and interests as the response level will help you determine what appeals your target market the most.

Twitter facilitates business users through search.Twitter.com where it is possible to enter your business or product's name to find out about conversations about you. You will also be able to determine if your efforts are headed in the right direction and responding in the same desired manner.

Your voice

Just be yourself. A lot of businesses try to be overly formal. A tweet is supposed to reflect your business's personality. Dry and boring tweets only send prospects running in the opposite direction. It is the friendly and conversational ones that are responded to most.

A Craft Beer Bar @BeerBelly_LA
Get out of the rain, come to BB, have a beer, grub on a Cheesesteak, watch some Monday night football... Welcome to the good life!

Give your customers something more which can serve as an added attraction. You can use Twitter to convey information or insights that customers won't be able to find anywhere else.

You should always be responsive to tweets. Make sure you reply when people tweet about you. Don't forget to retweet any positive messages and express your gratitude for those praising you. Similarly, you should address important tweets about your tweets at once.

'You can use Twitter to convey information or insights that customers won't be able to find anywhere else.'

There are times when you need to taken conversations offline. If the exchanges between you and a customer are becoming too specific, a good approach is to ask your follower to send you a DM (direct message). This will allow you to communicate with your customer via phone or email.

It is strongly advised that your download Twitter for your mobile so you can stay connected to all your customers on the go.

Making tweeting a habit

For all those who are wondering as to how many times tweeting each day is enough for a business, there is no specific answer. While tweeting once every week will be infrequent, you will go overboard by tweeting once every five minutes. Sound advice is to start off by tweeting once every day. With the passage of time, you will realise the amount and frequency with which you should share content for your specific business.

When it comes to Twitter, ideas work, no matter how big or small they are. Chances of business growth are endless and all you have to do is to thank a customer, retweet a positive feedback or simply enlighten followers about a happening in your community.

'When it comes to Twitter, ideas work, no matter how big or small they are.'

A common mistake is that since Twitter is a real time platform, it doesn't imply that it can't incorporate future happenings into it. Think of any upcoming holidays or product launches and try to find out what you can do to align Twitter into your plans.

A tempting tip is to retweet insights or comments or any news outlets or reporters covering your event. This way you'll not only be able to stir interest about the event but other reporters may be willing to follow you back as well.

Planning ahead on Twitter

Do you know that it is actually possible to plan your marketing strategy on Twitter ahead of time? The following is an illustration showing different activities you can perform to engage people over a specific period of time.

■ Monday: Special promotions – How about introducing some promotions exclusively for your Twitter followers? You can offer a certain code that will help your followers get discount on your offerings. You can offer bigger discounts for those retweeting your tweet.

- Tuesday: A look at behind the scenes – You can tweet any behind-the-scenes photos or videos as it will help develop interest in your followers about the way things are done.

Mayfair Theatre @mayfairtheatre
At the Mayfair, we still think projectionists are important. If you see Matthew, Markus or Nick, say thanks. pic.twitter.com/j8Vxtaqi

Hide photo

- Wednesday: Provide helpful tips – Make it your habit to create a series of surprising and informative tips regularly. Just be careful about the relevancy factor. As a chef, you can tweet tips for kitchens or recipes. As owner of a fashion boutique, you can share your opinion about vintage accessories or recent fashion trends.

Delta Faucet @deltafaucet
Need to clean your showerhead or faucet? Just use a 50/50 solution
of white vinegar and water. bit.ly/xkUHS

- Thursday: Create media spotlights – Use Twitter to bring to the limelight any
  news or stories about your business, community or industry that your
  followers may find interesting. Do not forget to mention the source or
  reporter when tweeting the story. This way you will allow others to identify the
  source with clear attribution.

The Charles Hotel @CharlesHotel
Mark your calendars for our #LeapYear sale. Save 29% on rooms
& suites. Thanks @USATODAYTravel & @laurably ow.ly/9figo

- Friday: Focus on profile – You can highlight people employed by your
  business. You can post their photos showing them working diligently.

Finding something worth sharing to tweet

Some tweets work better than the others. One factor that comes into play is that people are inclined to share tweets that answer a specific question, inspire, entertain or solve any issues. Studies have revealed that the most tweeted content on Twitter is one containing quotes, links, videos or photos. You may not know, but when you tweet something of interest, it travels to several prospective customers.

Attract visually

Using a photo along with a descriptive tweet can trigger many activities. It will be clicked and if it is worth sharing, it may also inspire retweets. For this reason, it is suggested that you think of your tweet as bait and photo as punch line.

Using Q&As

Your tweet can be in the form of a question relevant to your business and you can then answer the query in detail by posting a link along with it. For instance, 'Top ten reasons you need a new car? Answer: (provide link)'.

Sharing videos

You can improve chances of your tweet to get responded to by appending a URL to it. In an attempt to establish utmost convenience, links from websites like Vimeo, YouTube and other services play directly.

Adding a quote

You can easily impress your followers by using a quote from literature, history or anything relevant to your own industry. You can also give humour a chance by tweeting funny quotes about your business niche. There is no reason others won't retweet it if they think the quote will be liked by others.

While Twitter emphasises a lot about relevancy, you can always add people outside your line of business to get any ideas about engaging content. You can do something that has worked for them but don't forget to give the writer credit when you are using his/her content in your tweet.

Amplifying your impact

You can improve your reach and grow your audience easily with Twitter. The different strategies that can be used for this purpose are briefly described below.

Marketing your @username

There are a variety of ways you can promote your username both offline and online. It can be printed on signage, delivery vehicles, store fronts, websites, business cards, advertising, products, emails, etc. Whenever and wherever your consumers interact with your business, view it as an opportunity to make them follow you on Twitter.

Use followers to get followers

When your content is retweeted, it is actually you they are tweeting about. This is when you can effectively reach other followers. You can offer some sort of incentive. For example:

'When your content is retweeted, it is actually you they are tweeting about. This is when you can effectively reach other followers.'

CALICO @shopcalico
GIVEAWAY TIME! One lucky fan will win a $100 giftcard when we reach 2,000 Twitter followers! RT for a chance to win! #followshopcalico

In this example, the business has created a tweet that will encourage others to follow it. You can offer great discounts to every individual who retweets your tweet provide that his/her tweet gets retweeted, say 10 or 25 times.

You can offer your followers gifts for mentioning your business in your tweet. It does not necessarily have to be something big. An extra service, a free trial or a discount will do, depending on what makes the most sense for your particular business type. You can provide a link to a document specifying the terms and conditions of your reward.

If you are operating a shop, you can request your followers to tweet on their phones when they check out. However, if you have an online business only, you can always message the follower with the discount code every time he/she shops so that the voucher or discount can be availed next time.

Remember, when it comes to tweeting, people are more likely to tweet what they believe will benefit their followers as well.

Working with others

You can choose to connect with other businesses that exist by extending goodwill. For instance, look at the following illustration.

Kimbell Art Museum @KimbellArt
@SFMOMA @SFGIANTS Congratulations on your big win! http://ow.ly/i/5azl We were glad to be part of #museumball. What should we tackle next?

When the famous 2010 World Series was hosted at Arlington, Texas and San Francisco, California, it came as no surprise that there was an endless stream of tweets from both the cities. The biggest art museums in both the cities participated as well. The amazing Fort Worth's Kimbell Art Museum challenged the museum of modern art in San Francisco for a 'tweet-off'. Texas replied, using hashtags and mentioned both the teams playing baseball. The teams soon joined in as did the fans. Both the museums succeeded in finding common grounds of interest that gave rise to the competitive fun, making the game even more exciting.

Using Twitter products for promotion

Once you have accomplished the task of maintaining a productive presence on this social media website, the next step is the use of promoted products on Twitter so as to increase reach and score more followers. Twitter has a variety of services that help you reach the right people with minimal hassle to share your opinion, build community and encouraging old, as well as new, customers into staying with you.

Secondly, you can also make use of promoted tweets that amplify business messages by using options which makes it possible to reach the right people, at the right time, in the right place.

In addition, you can make use of Twitter promoted accounts. They can quickly upscale your business's influence. They are also taken into account in searches and appear in the famous 'Who to follow' section as well.

Measuring your impact

When Twitter is in question, you just don't sit around keeping your fingers crossed for things to work in your favour. True satisfaction comes from realising how successful you are. With Twitter, you can find out by determining the rate at which your followers are growing. Not only you are increasing your fan base, you are also facilitating them to connect to your business. Other indications you can consider when evaluating your success are:

- Find out if people are making your tweets favourites or retweeting them.

- You can use tools like Google Analytics that will help you estimate how much traffic you are getting from Twitter.

- Create contests regularly and introduce promotions exclusively for Twitter followers.

- Engage audiences by asking if they are following you and if they are enjoying your promotions or discounts.

By monitoring and measuring your influence, you can think of more creative ways to engage your audience and claim business growth.

Being an unbelievably effective advertising platform for businesses, Twitter empowers you to connect to those in your community, especially those who are interested to know what you have to offer. It is increasingly being used by businesses across the globe and using it will help you spell the kind of success everyone will talk about for years to come.

'Being an unbelievably effective advertising platform for businesses, Twitter empowers you to connect to those in your community, especially those who are interested to know what you have to offer.'

Summing Up

- Since being introduced in 2006, Twitter is now one of the most prominent and powerful social media tools around today.

- Although limited in size, there is no limit to the great effect well-constructed tweets can have on your business.

- Finding, following and interacting with the right people/businesses will help amplify your message and grow your business immeasurably.

Chapter Eight

HootSuite User Manual

HootSuite is a social media management tool. It is common for businesses to use multiple platforms for marketing their business and if you are looking for a tool to help you manage your several social media profiles or schedule status updates, HootSuite is everything you can ask for.

With so many channels of advertising simultaneously working for your business, one is helpless as to how to manage plenty of information via LinkedIn, Facebook and Twitter. After all, not every business can afford to have round-the-clock marketing teams dedicated to take them to the top.

HootSuite realised the need for a platform for the time-starved business owners striving to keep their companies right on track. With novel platforms enriching the web landscape every other day, it seemed as if any efforts directed towards multiple social platforms management would turn out to be a fruitless endeavor. In this scenario, HootSuite emerged as a sanity saver!

The atypical tool not only streamlines your business processes but also allows you to effectively launch marketing campaigns. HootSuite can lend several perks to your business. You can determine your targeted audience and make efforts to increase them. You can distribute messages targeted at desired demographics across an assortment of channels.

In short, it's fair to say that using this tool, any business can schedule its updates to LinkedIn, Twitter, WordPress, Facebook and several other platforms. You can keep track of your campaign's performance and can use industry trends to easily adjust tactics.

'HootSuite is a social media management tool. If you are looking for a tool to help you manage your several social media profiles or schedule status updates, HootSuite is everything you can ask for.'

This chapter will get you acquainted with HootSuite and its amazing features. In addition, we will also show how HootSuite can be used for brand prospecting and brand monitoring. After reading this step-by-step manual on HootSuite, you will have no trouble scheduling messages, tracking brand mentions, managing social media profiles, analysing traffic and a lot more.

Signing up

- Log on to HootSuite.com.
- Provide the required information.
- Click on 'Sign up now'.

Adding social network accounts

- When you log in, you will come across the following pop-up.

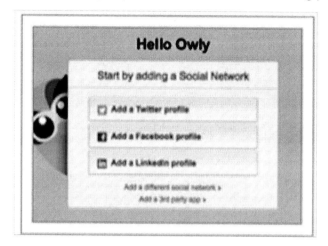

- From the menu provided at the left, choose the user profile icon.

- Under 'My Social Networks', you will find the option, 'Add a Social Network'.

▨ Next step is selecting social network that you wish to add.

▨ Choose 'Connect'. Just remember that for a social network to connect to HootSuite, it is important that you have logged in to the social network.

'HootSuite was built with the intent to listen to and engage your targeted demographics.'

Adding a stream

HootSuite was built with the intent to listen to and engage your targeted demographics. The following steps attempt to show you how to use your account on HootSuite so as to derive the best results from it.

Creating streams and tabs will not only allow you to save and perform advanced searches, but you will also be able to manage your followers, lists and filter content more effectively.

You will be able to see a 'Getting Started' tab.

- Here you choose 'Create a New Tab' and label it.
- Similarly, you choose 'Add Stream'. Now you can add content you will be able to monitor.

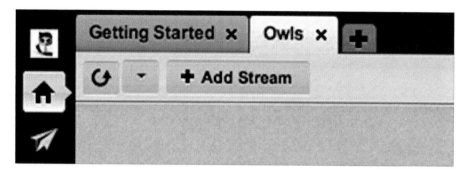

How to post a status update

Go the HootSuite launch menu. On the top of the left hand corner of your screen, you will be able to see the Home icon. You can type your status update there and send it on multiple social media platforms.

Compose and send a message

Messages allow you to create custom content which you can share with selected networks. Follow the easy steps:

- Click on the 'Compose message' field.

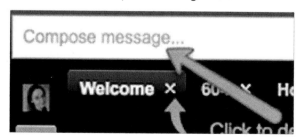

- Type your message.
- From profile picker, select the social networks you want to send the message to.

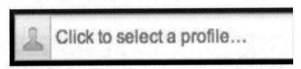

- Click on 'Send Now'.

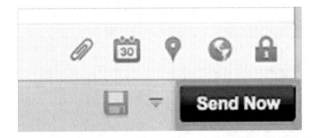

Replying, retweeting and liking messages

You can amplify user engagement through activities like liking, messaging, retweeting or replying your audience. This is done as follows.

- Hover your mouse towards the left, over launch bar. Here you can see several options. Click on the house (icon for streams).

- Now the next step is locating the message or Twitter user you wish to converse with. You use the reply icon for that.

- Once you click on the icon to reply, a new 'Compose' window will appear on the screen. You type your message here.

- Select the network you want you receive a reply from. Click on 'Send Now' and you are done.

How to schedule a message

There are times when we write messages but don't want to send them right away. With HootSuite, it is possible to write a message when you have time and send it whenever you want. Here's how you do it.

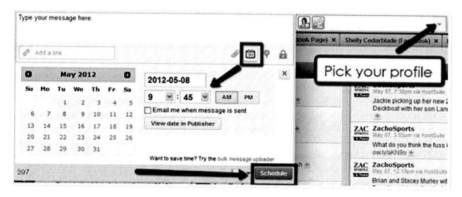

- Write your message in the 'Compose Message' window.

- Once you have typed your message, click on the calendar icon on the page. The calendar will drop down. You can choose the time and date to send the message from here.

- Next, you specify the profile(s) you wish to send the message to.

- When you are done, select the 'Schedule' button and your message will be scheduled.

How to edit messages scheduled in HootSuite

HootSuite understands that you may want to make some modifications in a scheduled message. You can edit it easily by just following the simple steps listed below.

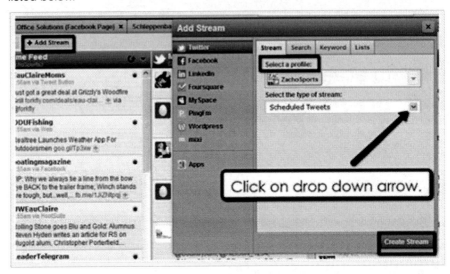

- Choose 'Add Stream'.

- On the left side of the 'Add Stream' option, you will be able to select a social profile such as LinkedIn, Facebook or Twitter.

- Select the desired profile.

- Now click on 'Select the type of stream', choose 'Scheduled Tweets' under it.

- Click on 'Create Stream'.

- A column showing all your scheduled tweets will be created. In order to edit one of the tweets, you have to hover your mouse over the message you wish to edit.

- You will notice a link to edit.

- Click on this 'Edit' link. You can change the message's content or you can reschedule to send it at another date or time.

- When finished, click on 'Schedule' or choose 'Cancel' in case you wish to keep your message the same.

It is worth remembering that the very same procedure is followed whether it is a Facebook message you are sending or a Twitter tweet.

How to add a link

Adding a link to HootSuite is quite simple:

HootSuite also has the link shortening facility. As soon as you paste a link, it appears as 'owl.ly' link. For instance, http://owl.ly/aLSO.

How to upload a document or image

'In case you do not already have a Twitter profile, it is suggested that you create one to post an image to HootSuite.'

- First of all, select the 'Compose message' field. Here you will see icon of a paperclip. Click on it.

- A pop-up will appear on your screen asking you to upload a Twitter profile of your choice. It is mandatory that you choose a Twitter profile to upload your photo first because of certain API restrictions. You can then choose the profile you wish to upload the photo to, Twitter or Facebook. Remember that if you want to upload a picture to your Facebook profile only, it won't be posted to your Twitter profile. In case you do not already have a Twitter profile, it is suggested that you create one to post an image to HootSuite.

- After clicking on the specific paper clip icon, a window will appear asking for the type of file you wish to upload. You can select 'Upload a document' or 'Upload a photo' depending on your content.

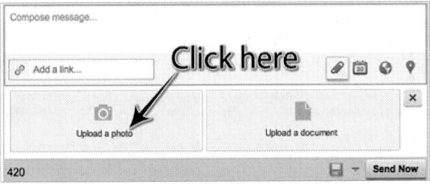

106

- Upload the desired document or photo and the upload status will be reflected by an indication bar.

- 'Profile' can also be selected from profile picker provided at the right of the message box.

Once this is done, a link can be seen in the text field for status update. This is actually the link to the photo or document you have uploaded. All files uploaded through HootSuite are hosted on owl.ly's servers. You send the status update and the specific file will be shared with several individuals on the social network.

This means that scheduling status updates along with complete attachments and links is no issue on HootSuite.

Adding apps to HootSuite

HootSuite gives you the flexibility to add apps. This allows business owners to incorporate some added functionality and features to their dashboard. HootSuite has maintained an app directory and you can get the most amazing apps such as YouTube, MailChimp, Tumblr, Instagram, Flickr and others from here. The directions for adding an app to your dashboard are as follows.

- Take your mouse to the launch bar on the left side of your screen. Select 'Tools' from here.

- Next, choose 'App Directory'.

- Here you will see the list of apps you can add to your dashboard. Choose 'Install App' apart from the app you wish to add.

- Once you have chosen 'Install App', you will be required to authorise your account. You can do so by adding your name and password for every single app you wish to add. Your job is done. Once the app will install, it will appear in your dashboard automatically.

Downloading HootSuite's mobile app

In order to allow users to manage multiple platforms more effectively, HootSuite for mobile devices is available. Regardless of whether you have iPad, iPhone, Blackberry or Android, the app works for all and can be downloaded from the app store.

In the 'Getting Started' tab, you will find 'Get the Mobile App', click on it and follow the instructions.

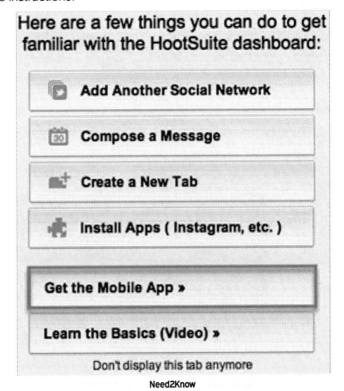

Need2Know

Quick tips for brand prospecting and monitoring

Now we are done with the basics, let's take a look at some quick tips that can give any business that much needed lift.

Search for product and brand names

The most common way of using a HootSuite search is for monitoring your brand. You can search specifically for product or brand names or any other terms relevant to your business.

You can initiate a search for a query including the name of your brand. For instance, if you search 'Louis Vuitton', you will get results for 'Louis' and 'Vuitton' but not always in the exact order. In order to get results specifically for 'Louis Vuitton', write a query as 'Louis OR Vuitton'.

It is now your responsibility to determine who's talking about yours or similar brands or businesses. Are people desperately waiting for your product launches? Are they telling others how amazing their experience have been with you? Who are the people excited about similar products or brands? You can reach these people and they can contribute to your business growth by dealing with you. The idea is to use any information you have to your advantage.

Keyword searches for brands

You can further make efforts by searching for brand keywords. There should be four to five keywords you should use for consistent brand optimisation. For instance, if you're an insurance agent in Leicester, you can use the keywords, 'Leicester insurance agent'. If you look closely, you may find people asking their friends or contacts, 'Do you know of any insurance agents? I am seeking someone I can trust.' Since you will be monitoring the conversation, you can jump right in and reach customers just when they need you.

'This but not that' feature

There are instances when we have a business dealing in specific products but there's a particular term associated with it that we don't want results for. Here HootSuite's 'this but not that' search feature comes into the limelight. You get results specific to your query with the elimination of all the unwanted results regardless of how closely they were related to the product or service searched for. Let's take a look at an example.

'Starbuck's roast coffee'

In case above, HootSuite gives users the flexibility to find all results for 'roast coffee' and opt out of those containing 'Starbuck's'.

Monitor hashtags

Keeping a close eye on hashtags is critical to keeping pace with ever-changing Twitter trends. A business can create and market them on its own. Let's suppose you have introduced an amazing £10 weekend sale. You can use the hashtag #10pounds for it. If you are doing it, say for a charity, you can add #breastcancerawareness into it, for example.

A common practice is of businesses using hashtags to determine people who are talking about their business or sharing information that can be of any value to them. What makes the hashtag an amazing idea is that it exposes content only to those to whom it matters.

Similarly, hashtags can be used to evaluate what's hot and what's not among your targeted demographics. You can closely observe conversations taking place and jump into them when the need arises.

If you follow any similar brand and can see that it's gaining popularity, you can find out what leveraged their presence. What made it possible for them to scout for the assortment of opportunities?

Monitoring competitors' tweets

Instead of just killing your time observing what others are saying, you should invest more time in finding out what your favourite brands are doing and how the information can be of any use to your business.

There's a lot more that can be discussed about HootSuite. However, for starters, this information is sufficient. With time, you will not only be able to get hold of the more advanced concepts, you will learn to maximise the effectiveness of your campaign as well. It is indeed an amazing platform to organise and manage all your social accounts. You can always stay ahead of others when it comes to posting and all of it can be done within minutes without having to hop back and forth from one platform to another.

Summing Up

- HootSuite is a social media management tool. It is designed to enable people and businesses to manage several social media profiles and update statuses on networking sites such as Facebook, Twitter, LinkedIn, etc.

- This effective tool helps save business owners time and money, instead of employing a marketing team to manage their social media, with some preparation and foresight HootSuite does the job for them.

Chapter Nine

Gaining Audience

So, you have successfully taken your business off the ground with the help of social media. You are satisfied with the constant stream of customers and a few weeks later, you realise that your competitor is raking in twice as much business as you.

You are worried as you just can't seem to put your finger on what actually went wrong. People love the one-of-a-kind ambiance of your shop that beckons them to step in. They are absolutely in love with your offerings. Where did you lack then?

The realisation hits you hard when you find out that it all started with a discount offer your competitor posted on Facebook. You acknowledge your naivety as you always believed that a social media presence was enough. Apparently, you were wrong and your worst nightmares have materialised as you see your competitor's business becoming the one-stop-shop for all *your* customers' needs.

'Social media is not just about being there for the sake of presence.'

Social media is not just about being there for the sake of presence. You need to win your audience. It is about inspiring enough trust to make customers buy from you. Something that was once believed to be word of mouth has multiplied a million times now, thanks to social media.

Can you believe that it is now possible to reach not hundreds but hundreds of thousands of people each day? Social media is not just any other advertising avenue. It can actually work wonders for you. Some steps that can help you expand your audience and take you a step closer towards success are as follows.

Promotion

Have you ever thought of promotions and competitions to engage and build your audience? With your marketing objectives and targeted demographics clearly outlined, you can use different types of promotions to enhance the influence of your social media marketing campaign. Some tips to ensure that you stay clear of all hassles when running these promotions are briefly outlined:

- For a promotion to run on Facebook, you need to have an app in place. There are several other guidelines defined as well but handling promotions via apps is the most important among all. Here you have the flexibility of having a customised app promising users a more personalised experience. Although Facebook does not offer applications for promotions, there are many free as well as paid third-party applications available which can be used. These apps are quite necessary because Facebook does not allow promotions and contests to be run directly on pages. Also, using an app for your business promotions not only yields value for your business but also helps you track the promotion's popularity and performance in a more effective manner.

- Promotions on Twitter require that the business provides the participants with a list clearly specifying terms and conditions. With just 140 characters allowed, this can come across as a big challenge. However, you can append the link containing the rules hosted on a separate web page in your tweet.

- You must be aware that lotteries fall within the government's domain and your responsibility is to make sure that your promotion isn't perceived as an illegal one. Anything containing a prize, consideration (such as a requirement to purchase or any other effort) and a chance in winner selection makes a promotion a lottery. Since a prize is unavoidable, stay away from consideration and the chance to avoid all sorts of legal concerns.

Now we'll take a look at tips that can help you build buzz with promotions in social media.

- Keep things easy and simple. Ease for participants can instantly spike your popularity graph. While this is not something someone will tell you, it is evident that contests that merely involve shares or 2-3 clicks are the ones to

'Bear in mind that long-lasting success comes from long-lasting efforts.'

secure the highest degree of user engagement. Motivate your users for viral sharing. Just make sure that you achieve the right balance. Too much of sharing may be perceived as spam which is something you will definitely want to avoid.

- Bear in mind that long-lasting success comes from long-lasting efforts. If you launch a contest and are oblivious to the happenings until the day the contest lasts, it's not going to get you anywhere. Don't forget to share milestones. Post updates about when the promotion is ending, the list of finalists and number of entries you have received so far. Use all of your social media channels. It is perfectly alright to advertise a promotion exclusively for Facebook users on Google+ or Twitter.

- Seek marketing partners for promotions. You may not even need to pay them. You can offer them exposure in return. Identify all influences and think of how they can be used to spread news about your promotion and reach new customers. For instance, if it's a photography competition and you know a famous photography blogger, you can reach him and convince him into becoming a part of your judging panel. Including his name will increase your credibility and the blogger's popularity.

- Another tip to keep in mind is that when you are introducing any contests where the users will be required to update content, a smart approach is to have some sample entries already in place. This will provide users with a good idea of what is expected of them.

- When it comes to judging, you can either ask users or fans to vote or you can have a judging panel to decide the winner. It cannot be denied that user-voting drives higher user engagement but there are often disagreements about the winner. It is, therefore, suggested that you have a judging panel for most of your promotions.

Handling promotions can be a bit challenging but companies of all sizes are using them to inexpensively engage and acquire audience, create brand awareness and ultimately trigger conversions and sales.

Commenting

When it comes to social media channels, comments emerge as a powerful influence. After all, it is comments where your audience expresses their opinion about you. They express their gratitude, approval, disapproval or disappointment in these candid feedbacks that have the potential to serve as a support system for an otherwise sinking business.

While there are several ways that can encourage your audience to comment, some things that can help you fuel the fire are briefly outlined below.

- When you are sharing content on social media platforms, try to share something that will be of interest to a large percentage of your audience. For instance, if you are dealing in accessories for mums-to-be, sharing tips on keeping nails manicured is irrelevant as it is going to be the last thing on their mind. Determine what will encourage your audience into participating.

- Make your content one of the best resources for information on your business niche. People will only respond to you if you give them something to value. People should be able to view your business as a treasure trove of authentic information they know they can put to their use.

- Use different forms of media. While people love to see photos, it has been explained before that on average, videos are known to generate more responses.

- When making videos, give your creativity a chance and don't forget to spice it up with a bit of humour. A little bit of humour works best.

- Comments do not necessarily have to be a detailed feedback. It is just response that matters. Even if it is just a 'like' or a one-word comment, you can pat yourself on the back as people are reading and taking interest.

- Do not forget to give credit when you are sharing someone's content. It is apparently one of the easiest ways to inspire comments. Not only do you get the approval of the content creator, if he/she has a fan following, they'll appreciate the recognition too.

- Ask for readers' feedback. Reader response is synonymous to audience engagement. The more people find your content useful, the more they will

'When it comes to social media channels, comments emerge as a powerful influence.'

respond to it. A clever technique, many businesses are asking for feedback, but make sure your solicitation is genuine. Using a custom request to leave feedback for all of your blog posts won't work for a long time.

- Commenting is a two-way process and indeed one of the easiest ways to launch into a dialogue with your audience. When you get a positive comment, acknowledge it.

- Leave thoughtful comments on content shared by your competitors and they will reciprocate in the same manner. If you help others grow, they will help facilitate things for you as well.

- Share content often. Doing it just once or twice each month will soon wash you away from the audience's mind. You have to stay fresh in their memory and this can only be done by giving your demographics something worth commenting on often.

Competitions

Competitions are valuable social media tools. With the rise of social media, there is a constant increase in the number of businesses who are now using competitions to outpace their rivals. The best part about competitions is that with social media, you do not need to make any extra efforts to make the competition known.

'When you get a positive comment, acknowledge it.'

Another advantage is that no matter how small the prize or giveaway is, there are always people who are enthusiastic to participate in it. These competitions are easy to follow and manage and using these competitions, you not only build your social media presence but boost brand loyalty among audience as well.

Five simple tips that can help you are as follows:

1. Assess your target audience by showing clearly who you are trying to attract, what you wish to accomplish through it and the prize that will be offered.

2. Once you know who to reach, select what the type of competition is you want. Keep your entry process simpler or you will annoy them. Have a simple entry form that doesn't require people to fill out lengthy forms.

3. After deciding the kind of competition that will work for you, you have to select a gift representing your business. The giveaway should be something inspiring engagement of quality audience.

4. When launching a competition, use the right channels to advertise it. Competitions on social media platforms mean that multiple platforms can be used in conjunction, which works in your favour.

5. Competitions are tools a business can use to leverage its presence. Make sure you maintain the momentum. Your brand shouldn't vanish as the competition ends. Keep on doing things to engage your audience and continue making efforts for your campaign with relevant content and conversation.

Make sure you keep all the points listed above in mind when launching your next competition. When done appropriately, you can generate more conversions and user engagement than deemed imaginable.

'Asking your audience to generate content is synonymous to success because you are allowing them to be creative and rewarding them for it.'

Reviews and customer content

Another audience-building strategy is writing reviews. A few years back, your opinion of a product or service wasn't anyone's headache. With the passage of time, consumer patterns changed and evolved into the idea that instead of wasting your hard-earned money on something that isn't worth it, it is only smart to see what others have to say about it to decide whether it is something you want or not.

Now people come to you when they know you are an authority on a certain category of products and that they can trust your opinion. That's why many businesses are now hiring people to write reviews for their products or services as it earns their brand credibility.

Similarly, encouraging users to generate content can also pique interest. Whether it is as small as writing a tagline for your brand or a 100-word description of any of your products, it is something that will always work for you. Asking your audience to generate content is synonymous to success because you are allowing them to be creative and rewarding them for it. This pleases your fans as they willingly participate to make your business vision a reality.

SEO – Optimising your social media

SEO, or search engine optimization, is a concept we all are aware of. This is a terminology used for all the collective efforts that are aimed at attracting as much relevant traffic as possible. SEO can work for social media websites as well. There are three basic strategies that will come into play here. If you aren't on board yet, useful tips to ensure that you drive maximum traffic for your business are outlined below:

- Try to participate actively on social networking platforms. Social media engagement is also one factor that search engines are now using to determine relevance and rating. If you successfully accomplish it, nothing can stop your business from getting where you always wanted it to be.

- Secondly, try to streamline your website so that visitors are able to share content, images or posts on social media. Do not forget to incorporate such features on your website. You will see the Facebook 'like' button or Google+'s 1+ everywhere as they are quickly becoming a standard. Also, people will share your content more if they are able to do it easily. No one wants to waste time logging in to a website, copying a link and then posting it.

- Finally, you have to take measures that encourage your visitors to share the content you posted with others. Smart business owners are those who know how to compel users to perform any action. Your content should provide value and you will soon be able to see it propagate through a variety of social media channels.

Smartphones

Research has revealed that smartphones contribute significantly to the traffic websites receive today. We are living in a technologically sound society where smartphones have entirely changed consumption habits. The prevalent use of smartphones has also given rise to user engagement and visitation of various platforms across the Internet.

The popularity of smartphones suggests that a business can amplify its chances of reaching quality audiences by incorporating this technology into its marketing campaign. Regardless of the kind of marketing campaign you are launching, just make sure you always provide the feature of receiving updates on smartphones.

Also, since the majority of the users prefer to access websites on their gadgets, make sure your website's design is as easy to navigate on smartphones as it is on a desktop computer.

Summing Up

◦ In order for social media to play a successful part in helping your business to flourish, you must use it actively in order to expand your audience and build trusting relationships.

◦ Using different types of promotions to enhance the influence of your social media marketing campaign can help you engage with and build up your audience.

◦ Use comments and feedback from your audience wisely. Listen to what they're saying – positive and negative – and use it to your advantage. Let this information help you learn what customers want, like and need from your business.

◦ Make SEO work for you through social media websites by actively and consistently using different social networking tools, streamlining your website so social media features heavily on it, encouraging visitors to share content and posts, etc.

Chapter Ten

Frequently Asked Questions

As we near the completion of this book, there may be some questions that have found their way into your mind. As an effort to be a comprehensive guide on social media for businesses, we aim to address all these questions. The following is a quick review of all the information provided.

Q. What is social media?

A. It is the collection of activities and practices communities of people use on the web to share knowledge, ideas, information and opinion. It can be thought of as a platform where people communicate and connect with those across the globe to learn and entertain.

Q. What are the different social media platforms available for businesses and people to collaborate?

A. Social media exists in many forms and some of the most notable ones are blogs, videos, social networking, podcasts, microblogs, etc.

Q. I am new to social media marketing. How do I get started?

A. Social media is not rocket science. You need to determine your business objectives and find out what you can do to accomplish them. Educate yourself. Creating accounts on different platforms can be a good place to start. As you gradually learn how things are done, you will be able to evolve your business and take it where you always dreamed it to be.

Q. Can social media really help my business excel?

A. When done properly, social media can be priceless to a business. Opening doors wide for opportunities, any of your business goals can be aligned and accomplished through social media.

Q. With so many options in place, how do I determine what will work best for my business?

A. It entirely depends on what your business is and the kind of exposure you desire. There are several aspects that can help you identify platforms that can work for your business. Every social media platform has pros and cons associated to it. By closely evaluating your options, you can make decisions to benefit you in the long run.

Q. How much time should I spend on social media to build my business?

A. Again, it depends on your business goals and schedule. Since every business and its goals are different, there is no specific figure that can be suggested. A recommendation is to determine how much time you can carve out of your schedule for social media in a week and divide it equally among days of week.

Q. How should I schedule my posts on social media?

A. As a business owner, you have to take care of a lot of things. Despite all efforts, it is not possible to take time out for social media every single day, and this is where HootSuite steps in. You can use this tool to schedule your posts in advance. Not only is it going to save a lot of your time but energy as well. The best part is that with HootSuite, the entire process is automated.

Q. What kind of information should I post?

A. Every business owner wants their social media page to be relevant and providing useful information, as it leads to customer engagement. The posts should be such that they encourage your followers to comment and respond.

Some things you can post are photos of events you have hosted, coupons, sales announcement, interactive questions asking for user input and tips and tricks on specific products/services.

Q. How do I find out if my posts are developing interest in my target audience?

A. Again, HootSuite can be used for this. It provides insight on the number of fans or followers you have on Facebook, Twitter or LinkedIn respectively. Also, there are many programs to help you judge the level of interaction. You can find out the number of shares, comments or likes you have received for a specific post. In short, you get a clear picture of the engagement level.

Q. How can I deal with spammers? Should I ignore them or report them?

Spammers are something almost every business owner has to deal with. If the comments are spam or there are posts saying hurtful things, you can simply delete them. People may incite you but a smart approach is to stay calm and composed when responding to anyone on public timelines.

Conclusion

For several businesses, social media is a buzz, a rage that is soon going to fade away. What these businesses don't realise is that social media is no longer an effort to go the extra mile. It has profound and long-lasting effects on every business. Neither is it going to vanish, nor is it going to lose its potential any time soon.

You never know, your business rival may be struggling to understand it while you were dismissing it as a luxury you cannot afford to invest your time and effort in. This essential guide has endeavoured to provide readers with up-to-date information to make the most out of social media. Equipping users with easy-to-follow guides, we hope to have provided insight into how business owners can grow their businesses while keeping their customers happy.

Social media not only drives results, when it is leveraged to enhance and facilitate social interactions, value is created. However, it is important to tread carefully. When used in the wrong manner, it can be a major turn off for your clientele.

Bottom line, use the invaluable and proficient tool competently and you will have no difficulty strengthening your existing client base and capturing the minds and hearts of scores of new customers.

Are you excited? A world full of business opportunities waits to be explored. Why wait? Dive in. Climb aboard the social media train today and start writing your success story!

Glossary

Advisory board
An advisory board is an informal group of local business professionals who can help you run your business better.

App
App is an abbreviation for application. An app is a piece of software. It can run on the Internet, on your computer, or on your phone or other electronic device.

Beta version
A pre-release of software that is given out to a large group of users to try under real conditions.

Blogging
A blog is a discussion or informational site published on the World Wide Web and consisting of discreet entries typically displayed in reverse chronological order. The act of structuring the content of these entries or posts is called blogging.

Brand awareness
The extent to which a brand is recognised by potential customers, and is correctly associated with a particular product, is brand awareness. Expressed usually as a percentage of a target market, brand awareness is the primary goal of advertising in the early months or years of a product's introduction.

Brand image
Brand image is the impression in the consumers' mind of a brand's total personality (real and imaginary qualities and shortcomings).

Brand loyalty
The extent of the faithfulness of consumers to a particular brand, expressed through their repeat purchases, irrespective of the marketing pressure generated by the competing brands.

Brand optimisation

An optimised brand is tightly focused on the audience you want to reach. When the brand is optimised, ideas, images and messages grab attention and compel response.

Broadcast
To send out or communicate, especially by radio or television.

Bulletin board systems
A bulletin board system (BBS) is a computer or an application dedicated to the sharing or exchange of messages or other files on a network.

Calls to action
Calls to action are words that urge the reader, listener or viewer of a sales promotion message to take an immediate action.

Collaboration
Collaboration is working together to achieve a goal.

Conversion
Conversion is the number of conversions your site or page gets measured against the number of visitors.

Corporate social networking
It defines the coming together of people to form a community of individuals where people interact on the business of some sort of corporate affinity.

Cost per Click
Cost per Click is an Internet advertising model used to direct traffic to websites, where advertisers pay the publisher (typically a website owner) when the ad is clicked.

Cost per Mile
Cost per Mile (CPM), also called cost ‰ and cost per thousand (CPT) (in Latin mille means thousand), is a commonly used measurement in advertising. Radio, television, newspaper, magazine, out-of-home advertising, and online advertising can be purchased on the basis of showing the ad to one thousand viewers.

Dashboard
In information technology, a dashboard is a user interface that, somewhat resembling an automobile's dashboard, organises and presents information in a way that is easy to read.

Demographics
Demographics are statistical characteristics [vague] of a population.

Direct message (DM)
Direct message (DM) is a private message sent via Twitter to one of your followers. You can only send a direct message to a user who is following you

Ecommerce
Commerce conducted electronically (as on the Internet) is called ecommerce.

Enterprise
It is used to refer to a business organisation.

Entrepreneur
A person who organises, operates and assumes the risk for a business venture.

Google Analytics
Google Analytics is a free web analytics service that provides statistics and basic analytical tools for search engine optimization (SEO) and marketing purposes.

Global reach
When people talk about the global reach of a company or industry, they mean its ability to have customers in many different parts of the world.

Hashtag (#)
A hashtag is a tag used to categorise posts on Twitter (tweets) according to topics.

Jargon
The specialised language of a professional, occupational, or other group, often meaningless to outsiders is jargon.

Leads
Enquiries, referral, or other information, obtained through advertisements or other means, that identifies a potential customer.

Marketing campaign
A marketing campaign is an activity designed to promote and increase the awareness of the business and one or more of its services/products.

Market niche

A small but profitable segment of a market suitable for focused attention by a marketer.

Mass exposure
The advertising, whether free or paid, of a specific product or service on a large scale.

Micro posts
Micro posts are short messages made public on a website and/or distributed to a private group of subscribers.

News feed
A continuous transmission of data, consisting of news updates, to websites through a syndicated news service provider.

Outreach
The process of an organisation building relationships with people in order to advise them

Page Insights
Facebook Insights is an analytics tool provided to Facebook page owners or platform administrators. Facebook Insights generates metrics that allow administrators to analyse trends about the activity on a given page.

Podcast
A podcast is a recorded radio-like audio program that is played on an mp3 player or computer.

Prospects
Potential customer or client qualified on the basis or his or her buying authority, financial capacity, and willingness to buy.

Relevancy
A measure of how closely a given object (file, web page, database record, etc.) matches a user's search for information.

Retweet
A retweet is when you re-publish something another Twitter user has written, to spread the word among your own Twitter followers.

ROI

For a given use of money in an enterprise, the ROI (return on investment) is how much profit or cost saving is realised as a result.

RSS

RSS is an XML-based vocabulary that specifies a means of sharing news headlines and other content between websites.

SME (Subject matter expert)

A subject matter expert is an individual who understands a business process or area well enough to answer questions from people in other groups who are trying to help.

Social interaction

Social interaction is defined as the way in which people respond to one another.

Spam

Spam is the use of electronic messaging systems to send unsolicited bulk messages, especially advertising, indiscriminately.

Sponsored stories

Sponsored stories are messages coming from friends about them engaging with your page, app or event that a business, organisation or individual has paid to highlight so there's a better chance people see them.

Syndication

An association of people or firms authorised to undertake a duty or transact specific business.

Templates

Document or file having a preset format, used as a starting point for a particular application so that the format does not have to be recreated each time it is used.

Tweet

A tweet is a post or status update on Twitter, a microblogging service.

Usability rules

Rules that assesses how easy it is to use an interface.

Viral sharing

Viral sharing refers to the phenomena where everyone who receives the message feels compelled to share it again.

Visibility

Visibility is the way you are represented to prospective employers and business connections.

Web standards

Web standards are a general term for the formal specifications and rules surrounding building web pages.

Word-of-mouth marketing

Oral or written recommendation by a satisfied customer to other prospective customers of a good or service is called word-of-mouth marketing.

References

Vertical Response. Available at: http://www.verticalresponse.com/social-media-marketing/faq. [Accessed on 6th December 2012].

Slide share. Available at: http://www.slideshare.net/HubSpot/small-business-social-media-e-book-hubspot. [Accessed on 4th December 2012].

Top Rank blog. Available at: http://www.toprankblog.com/2011/12/20-social-media-dos-donts/ . [Accessed on 3rd December 2012].

Social Media today. Available at: http://socialmediatoday.com/node/513583. [Accessed on 29th November, 2012].

Procon. Available at: http://socialnetworking.procon.org/. [Accessed on 20th November, 2012].

Go Gulf. Available at: http://www.go-gulf.com/blog/online-time. [Accessed on 2nd November, 2012].

Top dog social media. Available at: http://topdogsocialmedia.com/benefits-of-social-media-for-business/. [Accessed on 4th November, 2012].

East dev On IT. Available at: http://www.eastdevonit.co.uk/blog/60-web-design/170-astonishing-smartphone-usage-statistics[Accessed on 23rd November, 2012].

Copy Pressed. Avilable at: http://www.copypress.com/blog/5-lies-you-tell-yourself-about-building-an-audience-and-links/. [Accessed on 11th November, 2012].

Social media delivered. Available at http://www.socialmediadelivered.com/2012/03/08/tips-to-optimize-social-media-for-seo-build-streamline-encourage/. [Accessed on 13th November, 2012].

Everbill. Available at http://www.everbill.com/blog/tipps-und-tricks/social-media-marketing-2/. [Accessed on 21st November, 2012].

Chocolate shoe box. Available at http://www.chocolateshoebox.co.za/marketing-resources/using-competitions-to-boost-social-media. [Accessed on 1st November, 2012].

Social media examiner. Available at http://www.socialmediaexaminer.com/tag/social-media-promotion/. [Accessed on 9th November, 2012].

Strategic communications. Available at http://blog.stratcommunications.com/engaging-your-audience-through-social-media/. [Accessed on 19th November, 2012].

Webnox social media marketing. Avilable at http://www.webnox.com/viral_marketing/social_networking/. [Accessed on 25th November, 2012].

Hootsuite library. Available at http://library.hootsuite.com/Portals/125827/docs/hootsuite-whitepaper-8-tips-for-social-business.pdf. [Accessed on 22nd November, 2012].

Hootsuite help. Avilable at http://help.hootsuite.com/entries/21604477-adding-a-social-network-to-your-hootsuite-dashboard. [Accessed on 6th November, 2012].

Slide share. Available at: http://www.slideshare.net/pkitano/the-local-business-owners-guide-to-twitter. [Accessed on 17th November, 2012].

Global human capital. Available at http://globalhumancapital.org/the-unofficial-linkedin-users-guide-for-executives-and-professionals/. [Accessed on 16th November, 2012].

Social media sonar. Available at http://socialmediasonar.com/linkedin-user-guide. [Accessed on 3rd November, 2012].

CNet. Available at http://news.cnet.com/8301-1023_3-20084098-93/facebook-unveils-online-guide-for-businesses/. [Accessed on 8th November, 2012].

Business news. Avilable at https://www.facebook.com/business/news. [Accessed on 10th November, 2012].

Social media marketing girl. Available at http://socialmediamarketinggirl.com/how-to-find-your-target-audience-on-social-media/. [Accessed on 5th November, 2012].

Hootsuite help. Available at http://help.hootsuite.com/entries/21604477-adding-a-social-network-to-your-hootsuite-dashboard. [Accessed on 24th November, 2012].

Tech crucnch available at http://techcrunch.com/2012/07/31/page-post-targeting-enhanced// [Accessed on 31st November, 2012].

ROI revolution available at http://www.roirevolution.com/blog/2011/04/facebook_advertising_relationship_building.php. [Accessed on 1st November, 2012].

Inc. Com. Available at http://www.inc.com/guides/201101/how-to-build-better-business-relationships.html. [Accessed on 8th November, 2012].

Compukol connection. Available at http://www.compukol.com/blog/building-solid-business-relationships-using-linkedin/. [Accessed on 19th November, 2012].

Copy Blogger available at http://www.copyblogger.com/social-media-networking/. [Accessed on 16th November, 2012].

Hootsuite help available at http://help.hootsuite.com/entries/21604477-adding-a-social-network-to-your-hootsuite-dashboard. [Accessed on 23rd November, 2012].

Build a little bizz available at http://buildalittlebiz.com/blog/2011/10/31/marketing-strategy-build-relationships.html. [Accessed on 12th November, 2012].

Dummies.com available at http://www.dummies.com/how-to/content/how-to-create-a-winning-facebook-marketing-strateg.navld-610165.html. [Accessed on 2nd November, 2012].

Blue Glass available at http://www.blueglass.com/blog/the-right-way-to-use-social-media-for-outreach/. [Accessed on 14th November, 2012].

Cyentist available at http://cyentist.com/140-character-or-less-pros-and-cons-for-using-twitter-for-business/. [Accessed on 9th November, 2012].

Social for business available at http://www.social4business.com/twitter/twitter-pros-cons/. [Accessed on 17th November, 2012].

Dara creative available at http://www.daracreative.ie/blog/online-marketing/pros-and-cons-of-using-facebook-for-business/. [Accessed on 27th November, 2012].

Social media B2B available at http://socialmediab2b.com/2010/10/b2b-block-social-media-sites/. [Accessed on2nd December, 2012].

  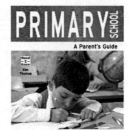  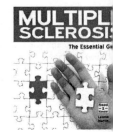